The Worship Hour

Pastoral Resources for Congregational Connection

DANIEL BAGBY

Also by Daniel Bagby

Understanding Anger in the Church

Transition and Newness

Before You Marry

The Church: The Power to Help and to Hurt

Healing Our Hurts: Coping with Difficult Emotions

Beyond the Myths: The Journey to Adulthood

Crisis Ministry: A Handbook

Seeing through Our Tears: Why We Cry; How We Heal

The Church and Addiction (editor)

Pastoral Responses to Sexual Abuse (editor)

Pastoral Responses to Suicide (editor)

Praise for
The Worship Hour:
Pastoral Resources for Congregational Connection

This book is an invaluable gift to ministers and laypeople who follow the Revised Common Lectionary. Dan Bagby brings the mind of an academician with the heart of a pastor, and what emerges are insights that will enrich all who read and use this book. I know Dan as a friend and a former faculty colleague. He speaks to where we live.

—Charles Bugg
Director of Coaches for Preaching
Center for Healthy Churches

If I didn't know better, I'd think that Dan Bagby wrote *The Worship Hour* just for me. As a pastor, I love to utilize my own creativity in crafting language for corporate worship experiences, but quite often that well runs dry. Drawing on decades of experience as a pastor and professor, Bagby provides his readers with generously thoughtful meditations, prayers, litanies, sermon prompts, and more. So valuable is this collection that it will not reside on my bookshelf, but rather on the edge of my desk.

—Daniel E. Glaze
Pastor, River Road Church
Richmond, Virginia

Smyth & Helwys Publishing, Inc.
6316 Peake Road
Macon, Georgia 31210-3960
1-800-747-3016
©2019 by Daniel Bagby
All rights reserved.

Library of Congress Cataloging-in-Publication Data

Names: Bagby, Daniel G., author.
Title: The worship hour : pastoral resources for congregational connection
   / By Daniel Bagby.
Description: First [edition]. | Macon : Smyth & Helwys Publishing, Inc.,
   2019. | Includes bibliographical references.
Identifiers: LCCN 2019022856 (print) | LCCN 2019022857 (ebook) | ISBN
   9781641731379 (paperback) | ISBN 9781641731591 (ebook)
Subjects: LCSH: Worship programs. | Common lectionary (1992)
Classification: LCC BV25 .B325 2019 (print) | LCC BV25 (ebook) | DDC
   264--dc23
LC record available at https://lccn.loc.gov/2019022856
LC ebook record available at https://lccn.loc.gov/2019022857

Disclaimer of Liability: With respect to statements of opinion or fact available in this work of nonfiction, Smyth & Helwys Publishing Inc. nor any of its employees, makes any warranty, express or implied, or assumes any legal liability or responsibility for the accuracy or completeness of any information disclosed, or represents that its use would not infringe privately-owned rights.

To the fellowship of friends at Seventh & James Baptist Church in Waco, Texas, who patiently worshiped with me and read my meditations for over sixteen years as their pastor

Contents

Introduction	1
YEAR ONE	
The Season of Advent	5
The First Sunday of Advent	5
The Second Sunday of Advent	6
The Third Sunday of Advent	7
The Fourth Sunday of Advent	9
The First Sunday after Christmas	10
The Second Sunday after Christmas	11
The Season of Epiphany	13
Epiphany Sunday	13
The First Sunday after Epiphany	14
The Second Sunday after Epiphany	16
The Third Sunday after Epiphany	17
The Fourth Sunday after Epiphany	18
The Fifth Sunday after Epiphany	20
The Season of Lent	23
The First Sunday of Lent	23
The Second Sunday of Lent	24
The Third Sunday of Lent	26
The Fourth Sunday of Lent	27
The Fifth Sunday of Lent	28
The Sixth Sunday of Lent	30
The Seventh Sunday of Lent	31
The Eighth Sunday of Lent	33
The Season of Easter	35
Palm Sunday	35
Easter Sunday	36

The Second Sunday of Easter	38
The Third Sunday of Easter	40
The Fourth Sunday of Easter	41
The Fifth Sunday of Easter	42
The Sixth Sunday of Easter	44
The Seventh Sunday of Easter	45

The Season of Pentecost — 49
- Pentecost Sunday — 49
- Trinity Sunday — 50
- The Second Sunday after Pentecost — 52
- The Third Sunday after Pentecost — 53
- The Fourth Sunday after Pentecost — 55
- The Fifth Sunday after Pentecost — 56
- The Sixth Sunday after Pentecost — 58
- The Seventh Sunday after Pentecost — 59
- The Eighth Sunday after Pentecost — 60
- The Ninth Sunday after Pentecost — 62
- The Tenth Sunday after Pentecost — 63
- The Eleventh Sunday after Pentecost — 65
- The Twelfth Sunday after Pentecost — 66
- The Thirteenth Sunday after Pentecost — 68
- The Fourteenth Sunday after Pentecost — 69
- The Fifteenth Sunday after Pentecost — 71
- The Sixteenth Sunday after Pentecost — 73
- The Seventeenth Sunday after Pentecost — 74
- The Eighteenth Sunday after Pentecost — 76
- The Nineteenth Sunday after Pentecost — 78
- The Twentieth Sunday after Pentecost (Life Stewardship Sunday) — 79
- The Twenty-first Sunday after Pentecost — 81
- The Twenty-second Sunday after Pentecost — 83
- The Twenty-third Sunday after Pentecost (Christ the King Sunday, Thanksgiving Week) — 84

YEAR TWO — 87
The Season of Advent — 89
- The First Sunday of Advent — 89

The Second Sunday of Advent	90
The Third Sunday of Advent	92
The Fourth Sunday of Advent	94
The First Sunday after Christmas	96
The Season of Epiphany	**99**
Epiphany Sunday	99
The First Sunday after Epiphany	100
The Second Sunday after Epiphany	102
The Third Sunday after Epiphany	104
The Fourth Sunday after Epiphany	106
The Fifth Sunday after Epiphany	107
The Sixth Sunday after Epiphany	109
The Season of Lent	**113**
The First Sunday of Lent	113
The Second Sunday of Lent	115
The Third Sunday of Lent	116
The Fourth Sunday of Lent	118
The Fifth Sunday of Lent	119
The Sixth Sunday of Lent	121
The Seventh Sunday of Lent	122
The Eighth Sunday of Lent	124
The Season of Easter	**127**
Palm Sunday	127
Easter Sunday	129
The Second Sunday of Easter	131
The Third Sunday of Easter	132
The Fourth Sunday of Easter	134
The Fifth Sunday of Easter	135
The Sixth Sunday of Easter	136
The Seventh Sunday of Easter	138
The Season of Pentecost	**141**
Pentecost Sunday	141
The First Sunday after Pentecost	142

The Second Sunday after Pentecost	144
The Third Sunday after Pentecost	145
The Fourth Sunday after Pentecost	147
The Fifth Sunday after Pentecost	148
The Sixth Sunday after Pentecost	150
The Seventh Sunday after Pentecost	152
The Eighth Sunday after Pentecost	153
The Ninth Sunday after Pentecost	154
The Tenth Sunday after Pentecost	156
The Eleventh Sunday after Pentecost	158
The Twelfth Sunday after Pentecost	159
The Thirteenth Sunday after Pentecost	161
The Fourteenth Sunday after Pentecost	162
The Fifteenth Sunday after Pentecost	164
The Sixteenth Sunday after Pentecost	166
The Seventeenth Sunday after Pentecost	167
The Eighteenth Sunday after Pentecost	169
The Nineteenth Sunday after Pentecost	171
The Twentieth Sunday after Pentecost (Reformation Sunday)	172
The Twenty-first Sunday after Pentecost	174
The Twenty-second Sunday after Pentecost	175
The Twenty-third Sunday after Pentecost (Christ the King Sunday, Thanksgiving Week)	177

Introduction

Every worship hour provides its participants with gentle opportunities to struggle with their dreams and hopes. People of faith and people seeking faith assemble during the same hour with multiple needs and varied expectations. Some worshipers want to recover a sense of purpose; others seek rituals of support and reassurance; still others listen for words of comfort and hope. Needs and concerns may differ, and sometimes they are not clearly identified, but people who come to a time of worship are usually hoping to connect, or reconnect—with a source of meaning and peace in their daily lives.

Worship participants listen, pray, sing, reflect, and struggle. Over twenty-seven years as a pastor in three congregations and almost as many years as an interim pastor and professor, I have listened to and tried to respond to the deepest needs and questions of genuine pilgrims in worship. In trying to care for their search and their questions, I have written the following meditations, prayers, and selected homily titles as I have led in worship over the years.

The following meditations of preparation are written for worshipers about to participate in the hour of worship. They are designed to anticipate concerns and questions in the worshiper's mind. The responsive readings bridge the questions with affirmations of faith, and the prayers are offered to express the struggles and hopes of the believer's heart. The chosen Scriptures follow the theme of the worship hour over two years in the life of the local community of faith. The sermon meditation includes a sample sermon title and suggested points to deliver in a message. These devotions can be used during any lectionary year (though the special days may not precisely align).

Introduction

YEAR ONE

The Season of Advent

The First Sunday of Advent

Meditation of Preparation

The silent sound is of a gentle Touch
That slipped into the hollow of our life:
The small carrier of an outrageous love that crossed
Every human barrier, to deliver us—an unimagined hope!
Listen again, to the quiet wonder in a Jewish stable . . .

Call to Confession and Hope

Leader: The people who live in darkness have seen a great light!

People: The people who have lost hope still seek the manger and the Way.

Leader: A restless people seek the child who brings us peace.

People: Joyless people seek the song that brings us joy.

Leader: A people dulled by work and duty seek again the face of love.

People: Make us ready for your transforming presence, Friend of hope!

Lead Scripture: Isaiah 9:6-7 and Mark 13:28-31

Sermon Meditation: "On Alert"
The importance of noticing the extraordinary in the ordinary, the value of being aware of signals toward revelation, and the importance of a "readiness" to see God's action in new ways

Pastoral Prayer

Do you dare come into our wounded, wounding world? Are you sure you want to travel our dangerous roads? Can you cope with our uncertainty, our apathy, our attraction to distraction, our shattered dreams, our shallow hopes? Please come! Do not allow us to discourage you with our anxieties and preoccupations. We really need to be saved, to recover hope in our helplessness, to know that you understand our perplexity. Come, child of goodness and grace, enter our imperfect world, and cause us to believe—again! Amen.

The Second Sunday of Advent

Meditation of Preparation

The truth is often found beyond:
Beyond the page, the scene, the words, the deed.
The truth is carried, never quite contained;
A book, a crib, a piece of bread, a jug of wine contain the truth
But point beyond!

Call to Contemplation

Leader: Here we stand, assembled once again, seekers peering through the darkness of a stable.

People: Lulled by the familiar, we yawn and sigh with boredom at the scene in Bethlehem.

Leader: We see no star, hear no angels, watch no miracles, offer no gifts.

People: Driven by the stress of the season, we are more the worn warriors of shopping than worshipers seeking a child that will save us.

Leader: Return us, O Lord, to the silent evening into which you crept to set us free.

People: Return us, Maker, to the stunning wonder of a birth that made the heavens sing.

Leader: Lead us by the light that broke the dimness of Bethlehem, and guide us into a purpose that makes every day a celebration, every evening an advent, every gift a joyous response to the greatest Gift of all.

People: Cause us to hear angels on high again, love in our midst, hope born within us—that Christ may do with us what he came here to accomplish. O come, o come, Emmanuel!

Lead Scripture: 1 Kings 19:11-12 and Mark 1:4-8

Sermon Meditation: "The Truth Beyond—and Here!"
The gift of looking beyond the surface, the call to see "beyond" the palpable, the richness of experiencing beyond first impressions

Pastoral Prayer

We come with small expectations to a place where miracles have occurred before, small Child; the story is worn, the anticipation pales, and our preoccupations mount. Have you come to save us from our sometimes pointless life? Do you really come in peace into our troubled world? Our hearts grow weary of the noise around us and inside us. Quiet our anxieties, we pray, that we may also be surprised by what you bring to our overextended ways; cause us to look again into the stable, because we've lost sight of what this manger child can do for us! Take away our selfish bent, our jaundiced nature, and our suspicion that you bring too little to our broken world. Show us once again that you have not forgotten us or ceased to care—but are at the cusp of our limitations to provide hope for today and peace at every turn. Come rescue us, Lord Jesus, we implore, for our sake and yours. Amen.

The Third Sunday of Advent

Meditation on the Uncommon

I seek uncommon things in common places—
I wish for unexpected value in the ordinary.
Do I seek voices in the dark? The sound of angels?

A striking revelation? An answer to the void?
Help me find treasure, missed before, inside a barn.

Call to Awareness and Joy

Leader: We are a common people with common purposes, O Lord.

People: We strive with burdens and requirements larger than life!

Leader: We strain to meet uncommon expectations.

People: We hold small skills and follow common goals.

Leader: Cause us again to unwrap hidden gifts you offer, see below the wrappings—

People: Touch the Holy, look beyond the average,

Leader: Pause in wonder, recognize the miracle

People: Of a child, our most uncommon joy!

Lead Scripture: Isaiah 2:2-5 and Luke 1:26-33

Sermon Meditation: "The Uncommon in the Common"
The advantages of valuing seemingly common events, the gift of recognizing God's work in the mundane, and the revelation of God in the ignored

Pastoral Prayer

We come as labored and heavy-laden people to the throne of renewal and refreshment! Here we look for lost priorities, search for superior road maps, seek to enrich our impoverished thoughts. Are there second chances in your kingdom, Gentle Child? Must we also bring gifts to receive the blessing of a lifetime? Will you receive us, poor as we are, and re-clothe us in heart and soul so that our faith is quickened and our joy multiplied? Wipe away unnecessary tears and show us the majesty of your amazing Presence, we pray. Amen.

The Fourth Sunday of Advent

Meditation of Preparation

Into the stirring emptiness
A child is born, who brings the sound of love
Into our cheerless hearts;
And all who hear the song will never be the same—
Will bow in adoration and in awe!

Call to Awareness

Leader: We thank you for the privilege of hearing your message of love, Dear Lord!

People: For witnesses along the way, whose love for you made them carriers of your compassion;

Leader: We thank you for names and faces in our memory that have shown us the gift of grace

People: And for a child who risked himself into a wounded world to give us greater joy.

Leader: Help us who have been touched by love to pass the message on

People: That others may find freedom and also know Your love!

Lead Scripture: Exodus 20:18-21 and Luke 2:8-11

Sermon Meditation: "Fear—or Love"
The complexity of faith as an experience of both fear and love, the power of love over fear, and the message of God's heart in the birth of love

Pastoral Prayer

We've come to thank you, Manger Child, for taking the risk of living among us! Greater love is not found than to care enough about our plight to visit us in the flesh. Thanks for reminding us that we can survive the inconsistency and emptiness of life down here; thanks for showing us that vulnerability can actually be a strength, not just a liability; thanks for infusing us with courage when we fear and cower in the face of many obstacles; lead us, Small One, past the wilderness of our shallow choices and unsteady hands, toward the calm that overcomes our dread of life and invites us gently into the grand purpose of your will—that we might rise with you and grow into your vision for us! For your sake, Jesus, our Friend and Savior, we pray. Amen.

The First Sunday after Christmas

Meditation of Preparation

I strain through every moment
Not forgiven in my past; I die a little
With the weight of yesterday. Yet still,
In every new beginning, I can live again—
Invited and released to start tomorrow
Without fear, and held by grace!

Call to Confession and Anticipation

Leader: We here return an unfinished year to you, O Lord of life;

People: We bring unfinished dreams and plans, untried kindness and care;

Leader: We ask forgiveness for promises we failed to keep with you—and with ourselves;

People: We come to be reminded that you accept half-finished dreams and deeds,

Leader: And that you cheer us on with a new year filled with hope and promise!

People: Teach us to make only as many promises as we can keep, still held as sacred plans;

Leader: Guide us to use memory only as an instrument of grace, to employ the present as a gift of love,

People: And to embrace the future as an act of faith!

Lead Scripture: Genesis 2:2-3 and Mark 4:2-9

Sermon Meditation: "We Sow Four Soils"

We are creatures of contrasting actions; each closing chapter is a chance for self-awareness and refocus; we can resolve in a new year to grow in Christian virtues

Pastoral Prayer

We come to you with our beginnings and our ending deadlines, Maker of time. Our hands are full of things we've tried, some completed, others still unfinished projects—as we ourselves are! Sift through our goals, dear God of wisdom, and help us dispose of shallow promises—made in the pressure of the moment but ill advised. Walk through worthy endeavors, and add your strength and focus to their finish, that we may find fulfillment in their labor, and in your will and blessing of them. Guide us also, as we begin again, to use good judgment in promises we choose to make, that we may be about endeavors that really matter, with substance and value in their content. Provide grace and a measure of forgiveness to us, we pray, with enterprises and vows that we must abandon; and bless us with good judgment, that we may be about your Kingdom's work, we pray. Through Christ, Amen.

The Second Sunday after Christmas

Meditation of Preparation

There is a moment in every intersection and event
Where things begin;
Unnoticed, often undefined,
There is a starting place, a birth
For all that will be. I need a starting place myself,
A birth of sorts, a promise—where I say:
I'm starting here!

A Summons and a Call

Leader: We are here to begin again, in some ways, Lord:

People: To make promises to ourselves, and to you—

Leader: Which we intend to keep!

People: In some cases, promises made before, soon forgotten or purposely abandoned:

Leader: Promises that will make us stronger, better, nobler.

People: Forgive us, first, unfinished deeds, never tried, or goals diminished.

Leader: Enlarge our vision of the future—and your work within us.

People: Enrich our thoughts, sustain good hopes, multiply our courage.

Leader: Employ our talents, shape our skills, direct our paths, Good Shepherd!

Lead Scripture: John 1:9-14 or Revelation 21:1-4

Sermon Meditation: "Promises, Promises"
The importance of making promises and commitments in life, the value of mutual accountability in such covenants, and the goal of raising our standards and values

Pastoral Prayer

Dear God of dreams and deeds, we are both anticipatory and ashamed! We are excited and eager to dream new things with you—but also embarrassed that we've made many easy promises and offered weak commitments. We need to know that you have not given up on us—that you will give us credit for wanting to do well, forgive us when we've failed, and encourage us to begin again. We confess that sometimes we wonder if we're capable of following, or even dreaming, distracted as we are by less important things along the way. Remind us, please, that you will prepare a way for us, will give us focus, and will journey with us—even when we falter.

The Season of Epiphany

Epiphany Sunday

Meditation of Preparation

There are causes and events that choose me and invite me
To become a different person; there are also places where I make
Bold choices, and define myself.
Such occasions are the births of covenants
With myself, and God: there, I become a different person,
Cease one way of living and embrace another.

Call to Reflection and Commitment

Leader: Who are we?

People: We are the people of God, called by his love in Jesus Christ to believe and to follow.

Leader: Why have we come here today?

People: To remember, to share our struggles, to listen, to reaffirm our vows.

Leader: What do you need?

People: Power to live an authentic life; freedom to be honest and open; courage to make good choices; faith to believe we can make them.

Leader: God is here as promised; Christ walks beside us to show us the way; grace makes it possible to follow.

People: We are creatures in a wounding world, dear Maker. Come to heal us. Make us eager to believe and able to love what you love!

Lead Scripture: Joshua 24:14-15 and Mark 1:9-13

Sermon Meditation: "Acting on What We Believe"
Assessing our capacity to add actions to our words, assessing what is a more consistent Christian life, and modeling the power of living what we believe

Pastoral Prayer

We're here to share our questions and our doubts again, O One who listens to our hearts. So many voices call us to so many differing allegiances, so many requirements crowd the corners of our mind; how do we choose among so many pleading causes? It's easier to sit back, overwhelmed by the weight of it all, and choose not to choose. Give us wisdom, O Lord, to choose wisely, to commit ourselves to what really matters, and to immerse ourselves with your priorities and plans. Help us find the capacity to make covenants, Good Servant of just causes.

The First Sunday after Epiphany

Meditation of Preparation

There is inside of me an unknown quantity
Left unexplored—and waiting
For the dawn. But will the day reveal
A hidden treasure? Or will it tell me
That I'm overrated, and have little
To offer an already impoverished world?
What will I find, and will I then be found?

Call to Awareness

Leader: We pause in awe and wonder at the magnitude of your creative gifts, so richly shared with us!

People: For shape and sound, color and form, taste and touch, fragrance and texture—

Leader: We take note, and give you thanks.

People: For memory and imagination, insight and reason, passion and compassion, choice and value—

Leader: We take note, and give you thanks.

People: For families who have nurtured us, friends who sustain us, communities that claim us, and Christ who still calls us—

Leader: We take note, and give you thanks.

People: For giving us a home, sharing creation with us, and asking us to make a home with you—

Leader: We take note, and give you thanks.

People: For Bethlehem, Nazareth, a call to follow, an empty cross and grave—

Leader: We pause, and give you thanks.

People: For bread broken and wine shared at a table—

Leader: Provision given and hope bestowed; we thank you once again,

People: And kneel, and hope—to hear your voice again!

Lead Scripture: Ezekiel 34:23-31 and John 10:1-4

Sermon Meditation: "Companion in Stark Places"
We have all feared that we are by ourselves; our deepest fears appear in stark places; God will shepherd us through very lonely places

Pastoral Prayer

We don't care what we've been told. Sometimes, we still feel all alone. Do you really understand what it feels like to wonder if anyone cares? Does it matter to you that we doubt and devalue ourselves? Are you really listening to us in the wilderness places of life? We'd like to know. We'd like to believe—again. Help us hear your voice above the howling indifference that infects our journey. For your sake; for goodness' sake; for our sake, restore feeble faith, Maker of miracles. Guide us through the rough places to green pastures, gentle waters, hopeful ways, we pray. Amen.

The Second Sunday after Epiphany

Meditation of Preparation

The call, at times, may seem unsure and vague;
The questions that remain are still profound—
And yet the invitation has been offered,
And somehow, somewhere, sometime,
In a definite way, we must each respond!
So—is this my turn, my call?

Call to Confession and Response

Leader: Here we are again, O Divine Maker—eager seekers and bored travelers.

People: Instruct our weary ears to hear new sounds;

Leader: Employ our blinded eyes to see new things!

People: Remove the dark of days gone by, the dreary memories, so that we may hear and see

Leader: Your voice, your call, your invitation to a nobler life!

People: Make clear the vision of a faith still vibrant and alive—

Leader: Remove ill chosen-paths, unworthy goals, ill-conceived routines.

People: Make every day a thrilling invitation to a promised place, where love prevails,

Leader: Justice is strong, and mercy shapes the causes we embrace!

Lead Scripture: 1 Samuel 3:4-10 and John 1:43-46

Sermon Meditation: "Call Waiting"

Each of us has a calling from God along the way; the calls are often first unfocused and disguised; God patiently calls us to a life of discovery, purpose, and hope

Pastoral Prayer

We confess that we have heard your voice before, Master Guide, and that we have turned away in fear and caution: we are not sure we can follow, and we struggle with what we may have to give up—to follow without pause! What will you make of us if we respond? Where will we go? And is it safe to follow? Can we trust you to lead us by still waters, to green pastures, where our very souls will be restored? Following is not easy, and we wonder about our capacity to remain faithful to your invitation—and in what ways it will change our plans and dreams. Give us the level of courage that will overcome anxiety and fear, and give us strength to follow when we know not where we go. In your good name, we pray. Amen.

The Third Sunday after Epiphany

Meditation of Preparation

What does he want with us—and we with him?
What will he take away? What does he plan to give?
Will we be better off—or stay the same?
And can we trust him if we do not know him?
And can we know him if we do not trust him?
Shed light into our darkness, Friend of light.

Call to Confession

Leader: We are a people much divided, Unifying God! We struggle between love and apathy, harmony and discord, commitment and distrust.

People: We believe, and yet we disbelieve.

Leader: We utter promises and praise, but our deeds spell carelessness and callousness.

People: We claim to love sister and brother, yet we neglect both in favor of our own concerns.

Leader: We salute good and study compassion, while we often practice harm and create enmity.

People: Yet we are the people you have chosen, and you have blessed us by believing in us, even when we fail to believe in ourselves.

Leader: You have rescued us from the dust of poor practices and have embraced us with your forgiving love.

People: Restore us, then, to the dreams you shaped for us; call us again to your vision and your purpose; and strengthen us to live up to your faith in us, we pray. Amen.

Lead Scripture: Deuteronomy 18:17-19 and Mark 1:21-27

Sermon Meditation: "What Will You Do with Us?"

God uses average people to accomplish good; sometimes we suspect that God is out to cheat us; God comes to us to heal and bless us

Pastoral Prayer

We come with heavy hearts to your place of healing, Creator God. We bring both faith and doubts together, unadorned, for your discernment. Sort through our stubborn discouragement, and renew our capacity to believe and to care. Bring courage to our faltering faith, reverse our withering hopes, and mend our broken dreams, we pray. Ignite in us a passion to believe—too soon forgotten; sustain in us a patience quickly abandoned; and spark in us a new commitment to your way and love, we pray, dear Friend.

The Fourth Sunday after Epiphany

Meditation of Preparation

Where do you take a broken heart?
Who is in charge of mending wounds?

There are diseases of the soul
That take me down and grow so old.
Is there a place where spirits heal?
Where broken lives can be restored?

Responsive Call to Hope

Leader: In this hour, O Master, offer us light for our darkness,

People: Courage for our fear, hope for our despair.

Leader: In this hour, O Master, give us peace in our turmoil,

People: Joy for deep sorrow, strength for our weakness.

Leader: In this hour, and every day, Lord,

People: Bring comfort to our pain, wisdom to our confusion,

Leader: And healing to our brokenness. Comfort and renew us, Physician of the soul!

Lead Scripture: Psalm 147:1-5 or Mark 1:29-34

Sermon Meditation: "Healing Our Brokenness"

All of us experience brokenness in life; God hears the cries of our brokenness; God in Christ came to mend our broken lives and renew hope

Pastoral Prayer

We need your healing touch today, Creator God. Our pain is not just of the body, but of mind and heart! We come with wounded dreams, diminished hopes, and worn determination. Anxiety controls our day, and night provides little relief from questions and perplexity. Can you remove worthless preoccupations and help us focus on what really matters? Can you sustain us in our uncertainty and bring peace to troubled thoughts? Restore our desire to care, and open our eyes to your constant work of restoration and renewal in this damaged world. Through Christ, our Friend, we pray. Amen.

The Fifth Sunday after Epiphany

Meditation of Preparation

We have no choice except to bear the past;
But how we carry what we bear
Shapes how we bear what's next,
For what we keep, preserve, or hold
Becomes a friend or foe. Do we let go
Of pain, despair, and hold
To faith and hope? If so, no load will keep us down!

Call to Confession and Affirmation

Leader: We have come to be renewed!

People: Our goals are dwarfed, our courage flawed, our witness faint;

Leader: Our faith wavers, our promises weaken, our resolve is unsteady!

People: We also come to be comforted.

Leader: We bear scars from hard days, hold memories of sorrow and listlessness;

People: We have suffered in places, waited, and even despaired.

Leader: Forgive us, Maker of life. We have taken good gifts and rendered them mediocre;

People: We have received much and employed little; wanted more and rarely seemed satisfied;

Leader: Yet you continue to forgive us, embrace us, and invite us again

People: To follow, heal, and grow. Give us strength, dear Friend! May we follow with anticipation!

Lead Scripture: Jeremiah 31:10-14 and Matthew 2:13-15, 19-21

Sermon Meditation: "Changing Mourning into Joy"

Loss and sorrow are realities in life; we grow discouraged in the midst of many pains; God remembers us and sustains us in our challenges

Pastoral Prayer

We follow, and we fail to follow, Path Maker; we start, then falter, then become preoccupied and quit; we mean well but soon forget our purposes and mission, and immerse ourselves into mundane and murky causes. Call us back to your superior values, and transfer our apathy into worthy passions for redemptive actions; remake our thoughts to fit your will, our steps to find your path, our concerns to care for what you care for! In your most holy name and way, we pray. Amen.

The Season of Lent

The First Sunday of Lent

Meditation of Preparation

Few sacred things remain; soiled hands too soon profane
And mar each reverent thought and deed . . .
And often leave a scar.
Is there no worthy thought? Is dignity erased?
Can life become abundant? Can secular turn sacred?
Can God step into vacant lives and fill the empty spaces?

Call to Awareness and Affirmation

Leader: We seek holy purposes—with tarnished lives.

People: We here affirm that life itself is sacred, designed with wondrous hope!

Leader: The world itself was made for good, for growth, for care and joy.

People: Each day is holy, every tree and river are a treasure,

Leader: Every human being an unknown marvel, every heart a noble enterprise;

People: Every soul is but a promise from the God of grace;

Leader: Every friend is just an opening flower, in the image of a Maker

People: Who creates in beauty and in care! Come then,

Leader: Let us love what God loves, treasure what God treasures, worship the Creator

People: And embrace and celebrate all that the Grand Designer made!

Lead Scripture: Jeremiah 1:4-8 or John 10:7-10

Sermon Meditation: "What in Life Is Sacred?"

We make artificial distinctions between what is "secular" and "sacred"; God designed creation as sacred and holy; we can worship and affirm and celebrate much of what God has made for us as holy

Pastoral Prayer

We've come to confess and heal again today, dear Master. We confess that we are distracted and preoccupied. There's pain and sorrow everywhere, and we are discouraged by our challenges and limitations. Apathy seems to trump involvement; faith is fragile; commitments to causes evoke more caution than excitement. Help us to recover a sense of what is valuable and sacred in this world; teach us to discover a peace that overshadows our distress; guide us through the shadows to the clarity that calls us to believe again! In your most gracious name we pray. Amen.

The Second Sunday of Lent

Meditation of Preparation

Around the world, where people ache,
Where hope is sought, and purpose made—
I see his face, I hear his voice,
And know he calls me to embrace
His cause, his walk, his gentle way.
And shall I listen—and obey?

Call to Awareness and Care

Leader: God of infinite care, we come before you, not alone

People: But in one another's company, and in the company

Leader: Of all your vulnerable children and struggling families.

People: When we share our troubles, and those of others, the pain becomes smaller,

Leader: And happiness and hope are doubled.

People: When we share other people's griefs and burdens,

Leader: Their weight becomes more possible to bear.

People: When we share our resources and our love,

Leader: Those gifts run deeper and last longer.

People: So teach us the power and the value of reaching out—

Leader: That we may be blessed as you are, in the giving!

Lead Scripture: Leviticus 19:9-10 and Matthew 5:1-10

Sermon Meditation: "Unto Whom Much Is Given"

We have been blessed with many gifts and opportunities; there is a divine invitation and responsibility to share what we have; Christ asks us to take initiative and bless the stranded, unblessed people in the world

Pastoral Prayer

Giver of all good gifts, we thank you again for the bounty you have allowed us in this privileged land, and for the privilege of distributing your gifts to others—that they also may be blessed! We have received much, and sometimes we are tempted to keep it for ourselves or hold on to all we have—in fear that we may be deprived or soon neglected. Teach us again the power of shared gifts and the joy that gratitude and giving evoke. Remind us that all good gifts come from you and are an invitation for us to participate in the exuberant and satisfying gesture of sharing from our abundance. May we give to others not out of constraint or guilt but from the freedom you have shown us. In your most holy name, we pray. Amen.

The Third Sunday of Lent

Meditation of Preparation

I stand outside
The wall, looking inside, seeking for him;
The wall is high, the distance wide
The door unclear . . . and then—
He stands beside me, by the wall, and now I know:
He is the Door!

Call to Affirmation and Commitment

Leader: O gracious Maker of the bubbling stream and blooming garden:

People: Have we acknowledged lately that the furnishings of earth are stunning images of your unbridled love for us?

Leader: Have we declared that we are still amazed at the detail of your creation,

People: The skill of your hand, the goodness of your heart?

Leader: Step into our lives once more, to complete good purposes and color vivid hopes!

People: Teach us to see the world you've made with eyes of mercy—as you do.

Leader: Show us new ways and roads untraveled, beaming with your promises!

People: Acquaint us with your spirit of gentleness and generosity—that we may learn from you!

Lead Scripture: Psalm 19:1-9 and Galatians 5:22-23

Sermon Meditation: "What Does Your Garden Grow?"
God has provided us with the capacity to develop "good" gifts in life; we often take little account of our role in "creating good"; God wants us to be intentional about producing "good"—as God does

Pastoral Prayer

Dear Master Gardener, we come again seeking your transforming touch and skill. We've sown poor seeds and let unhealthy choices and withering priorities take root. The garden you intended in our lives has too soon dried into a wilderness; we have not produced many good deeds; we need your tender care and loving work. Reset our lives to bloom in ways you plan; till the soil of our soul to bring your Spirit's fruit into full flower. Cause us to produce what you will honor: peace, grace, kindness, generosity, and love, that we may yet become the lovely garden you designed. For Christ's sake, we pray. Amen.

The Fourth Sunday of Lent

Meditation of Preparation

Disguised by prejudice and time
Eluding written word and rhyme, he walks,
Mysterious, into life; and will we know him
As he is—or miss him, searching
For another face? (Are you the One
We're looking for?)

Call to Affirmation

Leader: We have sought you, Nazarene! We have searched for you

People: In all the wrong places: we have looked for you in the comfortable and selfish corners;

Leader: We have failed to see you in the haunts of wretchedness and pain.

People: Through thresholds dark with fears, in paths where hide the lures of greed,

Leader: We also failed to recognize your voice and strain.

People: Where cross the crowded ways of life, where cries of loneliness abide,

Leader: You were already there, and calling us to join you—

People: Until all children you have birthed have learned to love, not hate, and follow

Leader: Where your steps have trod—to bring to earth the reign of God!

Lead Scripture: Jeremiah 31:31-34 and John 12:20-21

Sermon Meditation: "Seeing Jesus Again—for the First Time?"
Christ is so familiar to us that we miss the impact of his life; revisiting the Christ story brings us new revelations of the Savior; revisiting the person of Christ is to awaken a new commitment in us to follow him

Pastoral Prayer

We have found you—and we have missed you, Friend of the forgotten! We have searched for you and then discovered that you were looking for us. You wish to change us into your image and to shape us to your will; you want us to go where you go—in search of pain and sorrow, wound and neglect—and make our home where people hurt and fear. Help us heal from our wounds, that we may be healers ourselves; help us overcome our own fears, that we may follow without hesitation; help us learn to love ourselves, because you do—even when we fail. Grant us a measure of your peace, that we may share it on the road we travel. For your sake, Son of hope and Friend of many, we pray. Amen.

The Fifth Sunday of Lent

Meditation of Preparation

The world is a classroom for the smart
And dull; one learns much, the other little;
One is alert, profits from, and changes;
Another listens much but throws away.
What are the lessons that make living better?
Am I still teachable, dear Rabbi?

Call to Awareness and Choice

Leader: Worthy of being happy are those who express mercy;

People: They shall obtain mercy and be filled with newness of life.

Leader: God's tender mercies arrive every early morning.

People: They are expressed in God's priorities: to do justice, love mercy,

Leader: And call us to walk humbly with our Creator, for God's mercy endures forever!

People: So order our thoughts and deeds to also express mercy in our daily lives, dear God;

Leader: Rid us of the propensity to judge others and to see the worst side of issues and options;

People: Remove the need to criticize, and enhance our capacity to see the best in everyone and everything, that we may truly be about your image in our daily walk.

Lead Scripture: Isaiah 41:17-20 and Ephesians 2:4-10

Sermon Meditation: "Learning to Live as People of Grace"
Our experience in life is one of judgment and inadequacy; God's gift to us is a constant word of grace; in receiving grace our life is transformed and unburdened—and we can pass it on

Pastoral Prayer

We live with judgment and mete out judgment every day, O Divine Maker. Help us resist the temptation to see the worst in ourselves and in others, and open our eyes to better perspective and deeper understanding; forgive us the inclination to embrace the negative and accentuate the unworthy in our daily walk; enlarge our willingness to extend grace and offer mercy in our relationships; and press us to think and act as people of grace and hope! For your sake, and for ours, we pray. Amen.

The Sixth Sunday of Lent

Meditation of Preparation

What do you want with me, strange One
Who made the light and shaped the stage
On which I say my lines? Is the play rehearsed?
The story written? Every part assigned?
Do I own some freedom? Can I change the plot?
And whose story is it—yours or mine?

Call to Confession and Action

Leader: We stumble as we follow, gentle Guide. Confused by many choices, we hesitate

People: When we should choose clearly, not trifle over serious matters or spend ourselves on secondary pursuits.

Leader: We have often sought the path of least resistance, the road of minimal demands.

People: Save us from easy plans and cheap endeavors; invite us again to servant tasks;

Leader: Remove the shackles of our own preoccupations, the laziness that defeats us, the fears that paralyze us—

People: That we may experience your work of redemption in us, choose finer purposes, embrace higher challenges, and find the deeper fulfillment that arrives with serving.

Leader: Set our feet on lofty ground, gird our lives with every Christ-like grace,

People: And grant us your wisdom and courage for the living of today!

Lead Scripture: Isaiah 6:8-10 and Colossians 1:9-14

Sermon Meditation: "Too Hard a Path?"
The call to follow Christ is not for the faint-hearted; it involves changing attitudes, priorities, and ways of living; serious discipleship calls us to service and sacrifice and frees us to fulfill our true potential

Pastoral Prayer

Do you still want us to follow, Creator God—or have you given up on us? Can you manage our doubts and listen to our distractions? Will you guide us past our suspicions and pick us up when we stumble? Is there a limit to your grace, and have we exhausted your patience? Our doubts about you are mostly doubts about ourselves: we wonder if we have what it takes to serve and follow; we are afraid of being inconsistent, unreliable, unpredictable. Reassure us, if you will, that you can use us in spite of our frailty, that you care enough to forgive us, and that you believe we are still useful in your labor for a better life. Acquaint us with your peace that lowers our anxieties, that offers hope and focus to our scattered ways. Through Christ, our friend, we pray. Amen.

The Seventh Sunday of Lent

Meditation of Preparation

He passed by several times before,
While I, distracted
By what little I believed—ignored the invitation
And moved on . . . . Now, however,
When he stops again, I think I'll follow,
Just to see if there's more substance
To his invitation than the emptiness I've found.

Call to Commitment and Discipleship

Leader: Call us once again to follow you, Good Shepherd!

People: Distracted by the call of other voices, we've wandered into paths of apathy and self-preoccupation.

Leader: Teach us the ways that matter, and deliver us from wasted times and shallow findings.

People: Teach us the ways of hope, that boredom, selfishness, and prejudice may be roads avoided.

Leader: Show us the ways of peace, that all our efforts may be focused on your healing steps.

People: Free us from the tyrannies of greed, excess, and trivia; open our eyes to the narrow road:

Leader: The one that leads us to compassion, care, and deeper joy.

People: And may we soon remember that you always bring us food and water for the pilgrimage we take!

Lead Scripture: Psalm 40:5-8 and Mark 1:16-20

Sermon Meditation: "The Road Taken"
We all take roads that define us; roads taken for their ease actually have little quality and will betray us; the "way of the cross" is the most fulfilling and rewarding road

Pastoral Prayer

You've given us so many choices, generous God, and we often make such poor decisions! Breathe your sound wisdom into our minds and hearts, that we may choose in keeping with your will. Rid us of easy answers, shallow options, short-lasting ventures. Encourage us to seek the higher purposes and to embrace pursuits that bring us lasting joy and greater peace. Help us also shed burdensome anxieties that detract us from worthy enterprises. Mend our discouragements, and point us to valued paths that bless both us and fellow passengers along the way. Through Christ, our safe Leader, we pray. Amen.

The Eighth Sunday of Lent

Meditation of Preparation

I seek the form and face
That made this world:
I seek to know if Friend or Foe
Directs the plot or left the stage, alone;
I search to understand the mind
And heart behind this great unknown!
Oh, Mystery, reveal thyself! Unveil!

Call to Awareness and Faith

Leader: Stretch forth your hand, and call us into living, Lord of life!

People: Touch broken threads, and mend our wounded parts;

Leader: Touch broken spirits, and revive the source of courage!

People: Break out the greater purpose, bless our daily labor, fill our hands with eagerness to serve.

Leader: Renew our taste for challenge and adventure, our love for beauty, our desire to care.

People: Equip us to engage each day as active seekers and as focused followers, that we may leave this place as people of increased faith and deeper commitment.

Leader: Remove the barriers that prevent us from hearing your voice or believing in your grace.

People: Transform feeble faith, uncaring hearts, and controlling ambitions, and shape us again into the family of hope that every lonely traveler strains to find.

Lead Scripture: Psalm 67:1-7 and Acts 17:19-23

Sermon Meditation: "Recognizing God"
We have many early and incomplete images of God; many of our images of God are also inaccurate; Christ came to offer us the clearest face of God

Pastoral Prayer

We know you well, and yet still seek to know you, Mysterious One. You've given us a face and life by which we catch a glimpse of who you are, and yet questions abound: Are you committed more to grace than judgment? Are you still actively engaged in our broken existence? Is your silence punishment—or preparation? Will you sustain us when our pain or sorrow seems insurmountable? Do you really know us by name and care about the unfairness of human events? And will our struggles end and joy, someday, not die? Please answer from the mystery of your being, from your heart, and teach us how to live by faith when mystery remains, we pray. Amen.

The Season of Easter

Palm Sunday

Meditation of Preparation

He walks again into my life
And bids me walk away
From all illusions that betray
His truth! I stumble once again
Upon my fantasies—and pray
He'll lead me from their snare
To safer ground. Lead on, dear Hope—I'll try to follow . . . .

Call to Praise and Hope

Leader: Blessed is he who comes in the name of the Lord!

People: Blessed are you, O God, for you have not forgotten us—

Leader: Hosanna! Hosanna! Bring joy and hope into our gates, O Lord!

People: Come set us free, and give us strength; remove the clouds that block our view of you.

Leader: We thank our God for him who rides in peace—to conquer war and death!

People: Come save us from ourselves, dear Rider; we salute you, yet we fail to follow

Leader: Because we fear a cross and know what lies ahead.

People: Ignite new courage in our journey, and strengthen our capacity to walk beside you every day, beginning now!

Lead Scripture: Isaiah 50:4-7 and Mark 11:1-11

Sermon Meditation: "Faces in the Crowd"

Many in the crowd who chanted "hosanna" have a shallow view of Christ's mission; some of the same people shout "crucify him" when he disappoints them; Christ has come to "release the captives" of poor beliefs about Christ's mission, their life, and their salvation

Pastoral Prayer

We come again, as others have before, to regain hope, once lost, that you will work with us to quicken fading commitments. Like those who gathered years ago to sing your praises, we soon want too much from you, and disappear when issues consume us with discouragement. We are so tired of searching, working hard, and finding so little about which to rejoice or celebrate, dear Friend; please help us here and now to gain a portion of your gentle determination that quiets our burdened lives. Assist us also to believe again that bad days can end, and light and focus reappear—for sometimes we've lost sight of the path, or wonder if there ever was one. Can you hear the strain of our frustration and transform distress into a starting place for faith and strength? Help us, Lord of life, we ask. Amen.

Easter Sunday

Meditation of Preparation

The weight of all that hurts
Was thrown upon his broken form—
And he collapsed, and died . . . . But wait!
Apparently there's more! Whatever
kills and harms cannot destroy the Man;
He is not dead: He lives, and laughs at death!
And—can I do the same? Can death
Give way to life—and live once more, in me?

Call to Confession and Affirmation

Leader: We are the scattered believers who were gathered,

People: Once eager on Palm Sunday, then in agony on Friday,

Leader: And waiting sadly in the silence of the following day.

People: Then, at dawn, our hearts beat faster, and our feet begin to run.

Leader: Our eyes examine what appears to be—an empty tomb!

People: Remind us, Man of Calvary, that you often do your best when clouds are darkest,

Leader: That you also use the silence as a prelude to the greatest symphony you will compose!

People: Turn, then, our distracted eyes and minds from the turmoil of defeat—to the stunning victory of an empty grace!

Leader: Wipe away the tears of tragedy and sorrow, and brighten our today, and our tomorrow, with your sure and steady Presence!

People: Transform our waiting into anticipation, our apathy into eagerness, our lethargy into celebration!

Leader: Bring light into the dark corners of our lives, and reawaken every buried dream or valued dying hope!

People: Restore the quicker step, the flickering purpose, and plant a garden once again where deserts filled our soil—and soul!

Lead Scripture: Isaiah 25:6-8 and Mark 16:2-6

Sermon Meditation: "Fear and Hope"
Followers of Christ struggle with both fear and hope; faith is often overcome by fear and doubt; Christ conquers fear and restores faith and hope

Pastoral Prayer

Don't come down from that cross, Lord . . .
Unless you can dispel our doubt and confusion.
Don't come down from that cross . . .
Unless you can challenge our selfishness and apathy.
Don't come down from that cross . . .
Unless you can remove our fear and anxiety.
Don't come down from that cross, Lord . . .
Unless you can transform our small dreams and purposes.
Don't come out of that grave, Lord . . .
Unless you can give birth to new hope and better purposes.
Don't come out of that grave . . .
Unless you can bring a better peace and joy into our life.
Don't come out of that grave . . .
Unless you can resurrect faith and deeper love.
Don't come out of that grave . . .
Unless you can offer us a more abundant life—and save us from ourselves.
Don't . . . But please do! Amen.

The Second Sunday of Easter

Meditation of Preparation

Hopes rarely die quick deaths:
Instead, they slowly fade away and leave
Large, empty spaces in their wake.
So every day, inside of us, hopes die
A quiet death, and do we wait—with hope, again?
Or leave, and grieve, and never see the dawn?

Call to Wait and Hope

Leader: The cross is empty, the judgment seat is vacant, and the stone is rolled away!

People: Teach us, strong Conqueror of death, to break out of our graves:

Leader: The grave of empty dreams, joyless and worn with sameness; the tomb of broken hopes, abandoned and traded for inexpensive goals;

People: The plot of ground in which our promises are buried, discarded in favor of easier plans.

Leader: Roll aside the obstacles that separate us from you, from your way of life, your nobler path.

People: Empty our lives of all that needs to die within us, and fill the void with the light and life you designed for us, that we also may carry seeds of the resurrection!

Lead Scripture: Psalm 118:14-24 and Mark 16:1-7

Sermon Meditation: "Having the Last Word"
Life brings sadness and disappointment to places of hope; in places of despair and pain, our vision is obscured; Christ brings new hope and faith to us in our despair

Pastoral Prayer

Once again we have gathered around what we hope is an empty grave, dear Servant. We've sometimes been afraid that you're still in there—and if you are, our dreams and expectations remain buried there also. We've come to the garden with our own uneasy suspicions and our assortment of disturbing thoughts: Are our priorities ill placed? Is our anxiety a friend—or foe? Have we been busy with what really doesn't matter? Is our waiting for your help in vain? Do you possess the strength to draw us away from poor decisions, vacant plans, and a distorted focus? Can you bring resurrection to lost dreams? Please help us believe that you can, that we may live abundantly as you do! Amen.

The Third Sunday of Easter

Meditation of Preparation

I locked the door and ran
Inside of me; was running still
Until Someone found me, inside, locked in,
And wanting out . . . .
He called a dead man out; can he free me?

Call to Affirmation and Hope

Leader: The whole creation blooms and blossoms as you pass, O Lord!

People: The birds and brooks of water sing the wonder of your skill and care.

Leader: The sun heralds your Presence with radiance and dawning bursts of light;

People: Creation stands on tiptoe to behold your majesty and art.

Leader: May we, with nature, flower and grow lovely in your shadow.

People: May every thought and dream we hold, each deed and gesture, celebrate your purpose in our daily walk.

Leader: Remove the lifeless petals of unhappy choices, the withered joy, the shattered hope;

People: Restore the color and fragrance in our life, and from each budding promise bring forth worthy fruit, that we might blossom like trees planted by running waters, whose leaf and root will never fail, grounded in you!

Lead Scripture: Psalm 1 and John 15:5-8

Sermon Meditation: "Roots and Fruits"
Roots from seeds identify the source of what will grow; what we "plant" in our life has a lot to do with what we harvest; Christ calls us to plant worthy roots and bring virtues to blossom

Pastoral Prayer

We're here to confess our contradictions, Maker God: We want to trust you and follow, and we also do not wish to follow. We care, yet often remain careless. We believe, yet often disbelieve. We try, and yet we soon quit trying. Can you sort through our failed attempts at trusting, and accept us with our ambivalence and hesitation? Can you rescue us from the paralysis of procrastination and from the emptiness of self-indulgence? Will you restore our capacity to serve, to care, and to love what matters? Grace us with second chances, and call us to our full potential at the center of your will! In your most holy name, we pray. Amen.

The Fourth Sunday of Easter

Meditation of Preparation

I fool myself by claiming
To know more than what I know.
If truth were known, I would confess
That what I understand
Is even less than what I say I know!
I know in part, and that's a fraction
Of what I believe! I travel often
Through my memories, a seeker
Groping often, in the dark . . . for truth—and faith!

Call to Worship

Leader: We are, at best, imperfect followers of a resurrected Christ.

People: Christ called us each, however, to be faithful through our failures.

Leader: Accept us, then, O Man of grace, as creatures of imperfect deeds and incomplete reports.

People: Perfect our feeble efforts, heal our fragile faith, and quicken sluggish hands

Leader: That we may find again the vision we have lost, the path not taken, recognize your voice,

People: Believe again in what you call us to become, respond in strength to your request to care,

Leader: Rise to your level of commitment, walk a steadier pace,

People: And take the narrower road you named The Way!

Lead Scripture: Isaiah 42:1-4 and 1 Timothy 1:15-17

Sermon Meditation: "Good News for Wounded Pilgrims"
We are all wounded pilgrims on the journey of life; Christ knows our instability and imperfection; he came to heal our wounds, forgive our faults, and give us faith and purpose

Pastoral Prayer

We've struggled once again this week with our imperfect nature, Lord: We stumble, are easily distracted, soon discouraged, and always inconsistent. We've returned to be repaired, refurbished, and refocused; the places where we live paint luring and deceptive invitations. We are too soon seduced by voices calling us to focus only on ourselves, to take and hoard, to do whatever pleases in the moment. Remind us once again that easy promises bring empty returns, and that your purposes for us offer lasting fulfillment! Strengthen our resolve to follow in your steps, and grace each day with the assurance that you care for us even with our inadequacies. Through Christ, our Friend, we pray. Amen.

The Fifth Sunday of Easter

Meditation of Preparation

When did the awe and wonder disappear?
When did the stunning Presence fail
To jar our hearts? And how does something so unique
Become routine? What's more: How can
His startling form beside us once again

Disturb us to our core? Where is the insight
That causes us to pause, and worship holy ground?

Call to Reflection and Care

Leader: Find us again, Good Shepherd, in the dim cover of another solemn search.

People: We have been seeking clues to find the place of mercy;

Leader: We also seek the elusive source of inner peace!

People: You promised us a calming presence in a troubled world—

Leader: Our minds and hearts grow weary of the daily stress;

People: Apathy surrounds us, discontent assails us, and questions linger in the air.

Leader: Where can we go to hear your voice again? To find firm ground,

People: To follow safely in uncertain times?

Leader: Lead us again, Good Shepherd, since we are always lost and need a Guide

People: To show us a way through the wilderness—to higher places.

Lead Scripture: Psalm 23 and Isaiah 9:6-7

Sermon Meditation: "Can We Still Be Surprised?"
We often pay little attention to old stories repeated and retold; each truth and day provides events never before experienced; God is still at work to surprise us with more than we already know and believe

Pastoral Prayer

Surprise us, today, gentle Master—since we came in this place expecting so little. We've been here before and left disappointed and unsure. Our busy, often empty lives confess that there is something missing deep inside: we do not love enough; we do not care enough; our loyalty is shallow and our promises frail. Help us find the deeper meaning that makes life and labor more worthwhile. Remove our preoccupations, stifle our distractions, reduce our anxieties, and send us back into the week with confidence and peace, power and compassion, focus and purpose, all because you hold the secret to our hopes and joys. In your most sacred name, we plead. Amen.

The Sixth Sunday of Easter

Meditation of Preparation

I spend the day involved
But often unaware: Racing
Through life, I fill the hour, sometimes
Wisely—sometimes not. Is what I do
What matters? Is what I leave worthwhile?
Give me a clue, dear Lord, to choose what counts!

Call to Dedication

Leader: What a rich, equipped, and powerful people we are, generous Maker!

People: Rich in resources, opportunities, and promise; equipped to heal,

Leader: Provide, sustain, and strengthen many.

People: Teach us to share in the same generous way that caused you to give so much to us:

Leader: Trees, rivers, flowers, open fields, and multicolored canyons!

People: Lend us the purpose that equipped a people with a vision, a love, and the blessing of being chosen.

Leader: Call forth the gifts within us, as a chosen people, which reflect your image of grace and promise.

People: Grant us the privilege of blessing others as you've blessed us,

Leader: By giving lavishly, offering the joy of sharing our abundance with another,

People: And doubling thus the amazing wonder of giving and providing, for the benefit of all!

Lead Scripture: Micah 4:1-5 and 2 Corinthians 9:6-11

Sermon Meditation: "Hilarious Giving"

Giving and receiving are recurring actions in life; receiving has often been mistakenly identified with getting the greatest satisfaction; God wants to provide by giving the greatest and most lasting joy

Pastoral Prayer

We struggle every day between generosity and selfishness, O Giver of Good Gifts. We have so many wants, and quite legitimate needs, and we are sometimes overcome by the fear that we will not have enough. Yet when we step back and note the comfort of how we live, and what we already have, and what is at our disposal, we are forced to confess that we have much, and more than we need, and that you've promised to supply us in our direst moments. We also know that some of your children, brothers and sisters to us, worry every day about having enough to eat, where to sleep, and how to survive. Teach us the value of gratitude for what we have, and assist us in a call to give to others and to care for the least—as you care for us. Teach us more. Help us fathom the joy of giving and blessing another. Help us discover the personal satisfaction of multiplying your care by joining forces with you in giving of ourselves and our possessions to the family of God everywhere—because we ourselves have been touched by your abundant love. Through Christ's sake, and in his name, we pray. Amen.

The Seventh Sunday of Easter

Meditation of Preparation

Are we all bargain seekers
In the marketplace of choices?
Do I barter with light promises
To avoid the deeper plan? Do I invest in life
As little as I can? Do I target smaller goals
And seek the lower bar instead?
Is the comfortable and easy where I want to make my bed?

Call to Confession and Faith

Leader: We are the people of the covenant!

People: We have made covenant promises, and failed to keep them.

Leader: We are the children of hope,

People: But we have often sown more despair than hope, spread more grief than joy.

Leader: We are bound for the promised land!

People: Yet we are constantly distracted by attractive detours on the way.

Leader: Restore your purpose and priorities within us, and protect us from ourselves!

People: Lead us beside green pastures, to waters of peace.

Leader: Renew our lives through your Spirit and truth,

People: That we may follow, heal, and grow in grace!

Lead Scripture: Leviticus 19:33-34 and Luke 19:16-22

Sermon Meditation: "Beyond Discount Discipleship"
We have been asked to serve as disciples of Christ; we often seek the easy and the shallow path to discipleship; Christ calls us by example to embrace the harder, better, deeper service of discipleship

Pastoral Prayer

Rid us, Good Shepherd, of the temptation of the easy road! Call us, Friend, to understand the value of keeping promises, of becoming reliable followers, of being consistent servants. We confess that we regularly want to be served rather than serve, that we cut corners in discipleship and take detours on the road to spiritual maturity. Rid us of the arrogance that dares to presume that we are better than others who follow, and remind us of the grace that keeps us on the trail with you. Discard our selfish focus, and enlarge our capacity to care and risk the good. Teach us also that some pain is sometimes necessary in the journey of useful servanthood. Remind us of the sorrow you suffered in order to get our attention—and cause us to follow. With gratitude and hope, we pray. Amen.

The Season of Pentecost

Pentecost Sunday

Meditation of Preparation

Some events defy description
And refuse to be contained
In words or symbols; some occurrences
Live beyond our means to capture
Or contain them! They require imagination
To express the inexpressible:
So, have I just explained—the unexplainable?

Call to Awareness and Reflection

Leader: We gather once again as scattered people with scattered thoughts,

People: Seeking to find more than we have found before!

Leader: Our empty hands and hearts reflect a faith still yearning to discover deeper truth.

People: We've heard your voice before, and we must hear your voice again,

Leader: Or leave discouraged, disappointed, and afraid that what we know is not sufficient for the day.

People: Is there a Presence in the dark? A companion in the wake? A steady Spirit in the restlessness we know?

Leader: Help us to know that we are not forgotten, Lord, and that you care enough to remain with us in the fray and tumble of life.

People: Guide us with the gentle whispering of One who knows the path, has made the journey, and is certain to stay with us through every step. Breathe your Spirit into our dormant lives, Creator God!

Lead Scripture: Psalm 16:1-3, 5-8 and 1 Peter 1:3-9

Sermon Meditation: "Expressing the Inexpressible"
As creatures of time and space, we seek concrete evidence to confirm our faith; the Spirit of God is present beyond our senses and palpable evidence; it is by faith that we affirm and sense God's Spirit at work in us and in this world

Pastoral Prayer

The wilderness is large, and a safe passage so narrow, Gentle Guide. We have been lost before, and sometimes we grow weary of traveling and believing in the face of so much apathy and harm. Do you ever get discouraged with this world of selfishness and scars, where people focus on themselves—and no one else—and stagger through the day without meaning or focus? We need your encouragement, Maker of life. We need to know that you are still at work among us, present and involved, redeeming and rescuing, healing and restoring. There is so much that is broken or discarded. Help us work with you to recover your plans and purposes, to set straight the value and power of generosity and love, and to bring life where death resides. In your most holy name, we pray. Amen.

Trinity Sunday

Meditation of Preparation

I asked to see, and yet
Was really never blind;
I asked to know, and yet already knew.

How can I see, and be so blind?
How can I know, and still not understand?
And will I, seeing, finally know and recognize?

Call to Awareness and Worship

Leader: We've brought our lives into your presence for repair, renewal, and reorder.

People: Repair the broken strands of dreams, gestures, and deeds we have attempted in your name, O God.

Leader: Renew the hope, if lost; the heart, if faint; the vision, when it fades.

People: Reorder effort, to be spent in proper places; purpose, to return us to your priorities; patience, to provide perspective.

Leader: Re-form our hands and hearts, that they may be more fit for service; re-form our thoughts, to more properly contain your will;

People: Re-form our faith, to better contain your grace and love;

Leader: Reshape our choices, to employ your path and purposes,

People: That we may more perfectly reflect your way and manner day by day!

Lead Scripture: Jeremiah 31:7-9 and Mark 10:46-52

Sermon Meditation: "Wanting to See More"
Curiosity and inquiry reflect the image of God in us; pursuit of answers and discovery can expand our faith and understanding; God calls us to inquire, discover, ask, and explore in order to inform our faith journey

Pastoral Prayer

We are a narrow-sighted people, Divine Maker. We see, and yet we miss so much, distracted by our expectations, preoccupied by our assumptions, and blinded by our smaller views. We confess that when we cannot see you, we listen, but are too quickly mesmerized by the noises that control our concerns: our safety, our success, our competition, our possessions. We seek you in very few places in our daily run, consumed by our anxieties and driven by short-lived concerns. Help us see and hear your careful work among us and your gentle prodding within us, all designed to lead into peace-filled and fulfilling ways. Teach us how to recognize your activity and presence in surprising shapes and places; wipe away the obstacles from our vision, that we may genuinely recognize you in so many aspects of our daily pressures—and feel reassured that you are redeeming what we break. In your most holy name, we pray. Amen.

The Second Sunday after Pentecost

Meditation of Preparation

Do I suffer—by myself?
The silence, in the pain, is lonely,
Almost unbearable. Does anybody care?
I would endure the strenuous climb
If only I could feel and know
That someone else is there, and also cares.
Where are you, Creator of a universe?

Call to Faith and Hope

Leader: Meet us, O One who cares, beyond the daily darkness in the valley.

People: Assist us to the mountaintop, where you renew our souls.

Leader: Bring power to our weakness, rekindle our tired hopes and worn lives!

People: Sustain us by your grace, that we may here rekindle faith and promises we've made.

Leader: Lead us to believe again in ourselves, for our confidence falters.

People: Increase our capacity to trust you day by day, and to listen for your Presence in the busyness of our routine.

Leader: Free us from preoccupations and distresses that control our awareness of your healing care.

People: Empower us to become the followers you created us to be, and to engage each challenge with the assurance that you work with us in the day and into the night.

Leader: Bring calm into our stress and discouragement, and lift our vision to behold your higher purposes!

Lead Scripture: Psalm 86:1-7 and Romans 6:3-8

Sermon Meditation: "Finding Newness of Life Again"
Pain and harm sometimes erase belief; despair and apathy can often fill the void; Christ came to still the storm within and bring newfound peace and hope

Pastoral Prayer

Thank you, dear God, for your constant awareness of our concerns and anxieties. You listen when we share our struggles, and you listen to our hearts when we have no words for our troubles and hopes. Please sort through our confusion and bewilderment, and help us find meaning and direction here once again. We bring our fears to you, hoping that you can lay them to rest; we bring our sorrow to you, believing that you will sustain us; we bring our dreams to you, hoping that you will bless what is in your will and give us courage to pursue them. May your Spirit make us bold and useful in your work; may your divine skills sharpen our gifts and make us ready for the journey ahead. We pray in gratitude, and in your Son's name. Amen.

The Third Sunday after Pentecost

Meditation of Preparation

I am the captain of my soul,
The one who rules and has control;
I am the sovereign of my thoughts—
Commander of my hands and plans,

The author of all that I believe . . .
Am I, then, author of myself,
Or was I made to serve Another?

Call to Affirmation and Gratitude

Leader: We are a rich people at a lavish banquet, Head Master!

People: Brought to life under a beautiful sky, in a changing season, on a generous earth,

Leader: Called to use our minds and hearts in the discovery of worthwhile things,

People: We are regularly amazed at the diversity of opportunity, the variety of choices, even the many sides of love you have created!

Leader: Remind us here and now of the abundance of this graceful garden;

People: Awaken our appreciation for labor and leisure, play and purpose, passion and challenge;

Leader: Receive our heartfelt thanks for music we hear, color we see, compassion we feel, and touch that brings care!

People: Forgive us the casual appreciation of family ties, the glorious sunset wasted on distracted eyes, the loving gesture lost by inattention,

Leader: And bring us closer to the wonder of your Spirit moving through our lives to create reservoirs of hope and peace.

People: Work your miracle of Presence in our lives, transforming Spirit of life!

Lead Scripture: Habakkuk 2:2-4 and Luke 17:20-21

Sermon Meditation: "The Kingdom within You"
God's plan was that God's will would one day be done on earth; Christ came to declare that God's kingdom was "at hand" and within us; we are invited to bring God's will and way on earth through our actions

Pastoral Prayer

O One who inhabits the world you've made, and who still breathes life and purpose into your creation, please do the same with us! We long for the holy breath that renews our focus and our faith. We've entered your sanctuary seeking to recover the atmosphere and outlook that only you can provide. We want to follow your example of grace and healing, evident in every aspect of creation. Replace the inadequate thoughts and small purposes we hold, and transform our steps to reach more worthy and superior spiritual dimensions. Because of your Spirit, we pray and hope. Amen.

The Fourth Sunday after Pentecost

Meditation of Preparation

I seek to find a friendly Presence
In an often hostile world;
I seek forgiveness from Someone who knows me well;
I seek direction for my wandering soul—
I seek, hoping to find that which will fill
The restlessness inside—with greater hope!

Call to Worship and Perspective

Leader: Help us to know you in the mystery of worship, Uncommon God.

People: Incline your ear, and hear the private struggles of our heart.

Leader: Remove the guilt, provide the healing gesture;

People: Restore our sight, our spirits, and our aims.

Leader: Give to our vacant plans direction and commitment,

People: And teach us to respond with our whole life again!

Leader: So shall we then find wings for dreams and challenges to conquer, in your name;

People: Rise up, encouraged and equipped!

Lead Scripture: Psalm 138:1-3, 7-8 and Isaiah 6:1-8

Sermon Meditation: "The Irreplaceable in Worship"

Worship involves a mysterious hour for the encounter between creature and Creator; many of us bring preoccupations and low expectations that affect the dialogue; offering awareness, focus, and attention are essential to an encounter with the Divine

Pastoral Prayer

Will you surprise us still today—before the hour is done? Will you nudge us closer to a belief forgotten—or never recognized? Will you cause truth to stir enough within us that we will pause in wonder at the mystery we did not anticipate or expect? Can you still reach us, past the obstacles we've placed between ourselves and you? Will you remove the impediments and prejudices that dismiss your promptings, which tug at the edges of our heart? Break down the walls and partitions that separate us from you, dear Maker—and from love itself. This we plead in your most holy name. Amen.

The Fifth Sunday after Pentecost

Meditation of Preparation

I walk the fragile line of faith, unsteady
But intrigued, attracted to what might appear,
Dismayed by what has not been found . . .
Intrigued at times, sometimes content,
Fearful at others, seeking more!
Assist my find, illusive One;
Give courage to my quest, and show
The face I seek, beyond the veil.

Call to Discovery and Worship

Leader: We thank you once again for a community of faith in which to grow, Spirit of God!

People: Teach us the value of assembled worship, the practice of hospitality, the strength of fellowship.

Leader: Receive our humble thanks for friendships that endure the years, for faithful companions on the voyage of life, for steady witnesses in unsteady times.

People: Remind us of the rich furniture of earth, the surplus bounty that surrounds us and reminds of your care and love.

Leader: Grant us at least a partial understanding of the joy you feel in giving, that we also may rejoice in the exquisite experience of sharing.

People: Lend vistas to our imagination, that we may discover new ways and means to practice your love in the routine of our day;

Leader: And fill our hearts with your peace and fulfillment, that we may be full carriers of encouragement and hope to a distraught and disconnected world!

Lead Scripture: Habakkuk 1:2-4 and Luke 17:5-6

Sermon Meditation: "Growing Our Faith"
From birth to death, we choose what to believe; faith and belief are personal journeys each of us encounters; the increased complexity and challenge of living require the dynamic of an ever-growing faith

Pastoral Prayer

Today we pray for a troubled world in disarray, dear God. Tragedy and sorrow have struck in several places, and your children are suffering in many ways. Visit those who mourn deeply and without consolation over irreplaceable losses; sustain those whose dreams have faded; undergird frail stamina and vacillating courage; direct our path to opportunities of ministry and healing, and teach us to walk with patience into the work of care and recovery. Instruct us also on how to make a difference in a world of physical and spiritual hunger, confusion, homelessness, and fear. Equip us with your grace and care, that we may carry your good news to those who need it most. Through Christ we pray. Amen.

The Sixth Sunday after Pentecost

Meditation of Preparation

So many seeds, unknown, are sown
But never grow; so many gardens live
And blossom—only in my mind.
So many visions bloom, and prosper
Until tried. So many things to do, so many
Dreams to try: And will they live—or die?

Call to Awareness and Growth

Leader: We are the garden you created, Master Gardener!

People: Adorned as well as lilies of the field, we marvel at the detail of your work.

Leader: And, as flowers thirst for water, we raise our hands and hearts in hope

People: That you will pour upon us life-sustaining gifts, renew our spirits, energize our growth.

Leader: We confess that on our own we wither, lose vitality, discolor,

People: And return to you unfilled, and unfulfilled. Restore the ray of light that illumines the way, shower our dreams with hope, and strengthen weary roots.

Leader: Return the color to our goals, the bloom to our resolve, the beauty to our deeds—

People: That we may flower as a garden in the wilderness we've made!

Lead Scripture: Isaiah 55:10-11 and Luke 8:4-5

Sermon Meditation: "Helping Good Things Grow"
Our lives hold a diversity of soils; some of our soil offers good growth, but some provides poor sustenance; Christ calls us to provide good soil to bring God's purposes to full fruition

Pastoral Prayer

We come to you seeking the water of life, dear One. You've planted worthy deeds, watered sacred hopes, and gently cared for us in every season; and yet we return to you unkempt, somewhat withered, and without proper care. Replenish purpose and determination in our lives, we pray. We've been distracted once again by the surprises and challenges in each turn of the road, and our capacity to recover and choose wisely is damaged. Remake the garden you intended in us when you started, and prune away what interferes with your grand purpose for us, that we may grow in grace and peace, and in your will! Amen.

The Seventh Sunday after Pentecost

Meditation of Preparation

My soul, in search of one safe place,
Wanders through corners pressed, afraid.
Is there a shelter from the storm? A place to lean,
When tired and torn?
A holy ground—a place called home?
Is there a candle in the dark?

Call to Shelter and Care

Leader: We know that God is our shelter and strength,

People: A certain help in every trouble; we will not fear, therefore,

Leader: When the earth begins to tremble, and our surroundings shake;

People: When weak foundations crumble, and our hearts begin to quiver;

Leader: Because there is a river from God whose streams make us glad,

People: Whose power sustains us in any storm, for God is in the midst of her.

Leader: We will not fail; God will prevail, for the God of Jacob is our fortress.

People: Come, let us find a firm and unshakable refuge in the shadow of the Almighty! (Adapted from Psalm 46)

Lead Scripture: 2 Kings 4:8-13, Luke 10:38, and John 14:22-26

Sermon Meditation: "A Place for You"
We live as pilgrims seeking a "spiritual" home; "home" is where we find safety, meaning, love, and joy to share; Christ invites us to "make our home" with him

Pastoral Prayer

We seek protection from a dangerous and harming world, O God. Callousness and violence overcome peace and safety every day, and we feel more vulnerable and unprotected than ever. Where can we go to find safety, and to join forces with gentleness and peace? Remind us, when we forget, that your Son faced harm and injury each day he shared with us, and that you understand how dangerously we can live when we forget to live by your principles and priorities. Assist us in the task of taming anger so that it is not destructive, and in directing our passions to produce good deeds and helpful outcomes, not only in ourselves but also with our neighbors. Give us your wisdom, Author of Every Good. Amen.

The Eighth Sunday after Pentecost

Meditation of Preparation

What shall I do now that he's gone?
My courage stems from what I see and touch—
How can I walk the journey with no guide?
How can I follow when I know not where to go?
The risk is great, the path untried, the future dim.
I need a hand, a word, a plan;
Are you still out there, and here beside me, Shepherd Lord?

Call to Worship and Faith

Leader: With shadows and distress surrounding us, we gather to find light and hope anew!

People: Dark colors paint the lives of people wounded by sorrow, betrayed by circumstances, surprised by sudden tragedy and loss;

Leader: Yet you, Beacon of Light, command the darkness, shape horizons, dispel gloom, and bid the dimness vanish, conquered by your revealing Presence!

People: Call forth the calm that covers every soul with peace; evoke the confidence that quenches every fear; remove the clouds, and breathe your Spirit into every vacant corner and awaiting heart.

Leader: Return, O God who never quits and never leaves us to our own designs: reset our course to meet the Risen Lord—

People: Remain the One who cares when others falter, guide us through whatever dismal days assail us, and give us strength and courage to love and live more deeply than we ever have before!

Lead Scripture: Exodus 33:12-17 and Luke 24:46-53

Sermon Meditation: "Now What?"
Each new day offers unknown and unexpected events; to start the day—and any season—requires faith; Christ invites us to live by faith into an unrehearsed tomorrow

Pastoral Prayer

You have called us to a promised land where life is superior and sacred, and we've come to join you in the pilgrimage to find it, Shepherd God. You also know that we quite soon are lost and wandering in the desert; we struggle with our own inadequacies, our anxieties about the unknown, and our concern that we are not capable of becoming the disciples you need. We strive to do well, but fail so often; our generosity soon becomes selfishness, and our gratitude turns quickly to complaint. Can you redeem incomplete oaths and half-hearted commitments? Can you hold us up at the weak places and sustain us during our apprehensions? If you can, then you give birth to hope again within us, and we can pledge to follow by your grace. So be it, Maker of the Promised Path. Amen.

The Ninth Sunday after Pentecost

Meditation of Preparation

Sometimes irrelevant, sometimes uninvolved;
Sometimes caring, often fearful,
Yet concerned to make a difference;
Sometimes bewildered, sometimes preoccupied
Or easily distracted; sometimes willing, eager, helpful,
And courageous! Sometimes, but not often,
I am even useful—in this careless world.

Call to Faith and Community

Leader: We have assembled once again to remember that we are not alone!

People: We have a God who loves us, and a family of friends who surround us with care.

Leader: Help us here and now to understand what it means to be believed in, to belong to family, to be trusted by others!

Leader: Call us then to form friendships and family with those who grace our path each day.

People: Assist us in your purpose for forming ties of community and trust between people, and quicken our gestures of care and interest in your children near and far.

Leader: Remind us that your abundant living was not just for ourselves, but for all people, and that your promises of love and care were to extend to everyone.

People: Rekindle our interest in justice, mercy, compassion, service, and genuine love.

Leader: Remove careless habits, wasted efforts, shallow aspirations, and useless living.

People: Inhabit our hearts, govern our hands, and clothe our deeds with your grace and Spirit, that we may with integrity and initiative become the family of God on earth!

Lead Scripture: Jonah 4:5-11 and Luke 13:6-9

Sermon Meditation: "The Useful Life"
We have the freedom to choose daily what to do and how to spend our energy; some of our choices and efforts are wasteful, some of little value; God has called us to a useful stewardship of time and opportunity

Pastoral Prayer

We come to you overpowered and overwhelmed by the requirements of our journey, Creator God. We struggle with the weight of important decisions, divided loyalties, unhappy choices, and challenging relationships. Do you know the heaviness of too much labor—and too few resources? Can you understand the discouragement that entertains the possibility of giving up? Can you help us when we don't know what to do next? Please walk gently into our anxious thoughts, and dissipate unnecessary worries. Assist us with wisdom to choose what is best; grant us the grace to release burdens too large to bear and the patience to make choices that provide peace and don't require perfection. Teach us also how to rest and measure success in worthy ways. For our sake, and for your will to be done in our lives, we pray. Amen.

The Tenth Sunday after Pentecost

Meditation of Preparation

I stumble, pause, believe, then doubt
What I believed before;
I wonder, question, doubt my doubts—
Then trust my hopes once more . . . .

I am an honest pilgrim in a troubled world.
Can doubt become for me a step toward faith?

Call to Question and Commitment

Leader: God, we gather to celebrate the unfathomable dimension of your nature,

People: The wonder of your grace, the depth of your love, the magnitude of your creation!

Leader: The mystery of your presence among us is a source of amazement.

People: The reality of forgiveness is an incredible gesture.

Leader: The possibility of your guidance and wisdom is a certain reassurance!

People: Your encouragement and nurture provide us strength for every challenge.

Leader: You offer resurrection today to dormant dreams and feeble purposes.

People: So call us here and now, again, to all that you imagined at creation we'd become, so that we may respond to your high standards for us!

Lead Scripture: Psalm 22:1-11 and Mark 9:14-24

Sermon Meditation: "Belief and Unbelief"
Daily events elicit both faith and doubt; we struggle with hope and fear, faith and doubt, in important personal moments; Christ can work with the smallest vestige of faith to increase our capacity to believe and follow him

Pastoral Prayer

How odd it seems that we are creatures who believe, yet we fail in faith each day, Holy Guide. We find some comfort that some of your best-known followers also struggled with their faith: Abraham, Moses, Elijah, and Jonah are brothers to our doubts and disbelief, we know. You welcomed the father of an epileptic to believe further, and more; do the same with us, we pray. Sometimes we know we ask for things that are not wise. We also recognize that some petitions take much time to blossom, and our impatience often is an issue in our battle with belief. Give us, then, dear Maker, a double measure of your peace and confidence, that we may bring our greatest stirrings to you and trust you with what we cannot understand or see. Increase our faith, Shepherd of the flock! Amen.

The Eleventh Sunday after Pentecost

Meditation of Preparation

Each day I touch the frail and human side
Of life; each day the shadows work to overcome
The dawn; each day the gentle hand of God
Moves out to touch the trembling hand I stretch;
Each day the human must encounter the divine!

Call to Affirmation and Worship

Leader: We have entered this sacred space in hopes that we may be found out:

People: Found out and still accepted, we hope. We have come from the safety of our hiddenness

Leader: To plead for the refreshing openness by which your grace receives us as we are!

People: We lead imperfect lives, and we plead again for your wisdom and direction when we lose the way.

Leader: You know our faults and can bring healing and renewal to our worn ambitions.

People: You understand our pain and can provide relief and comfort in our disappointments.

Leader: You also offer a superior path to our self-focused preferences.

People: Refurbish our untended priorities to fit your will and wisdom, and plant our feet on higher ground and worthier ways!

Lead Scripture: Psalm 116:16-19 and Mark 8:31-33

Sermon Meditation: "The Perfect and Imperfect"
God has chosen in history to work with imperfection; we are each imperfect followers and people; God can deliver good news even through our imperfections

Pastoral Prayer

Restore us, Almighty God, to the vision and path you prepared from the beginning! Rid us of the notion that we know more than you do and that our choices without you are adequate and best. Return us to the higher ground, and help us see the abundance in your plans for us, and the joy you intend for this pilgrimage! Too soon we tire of believing and following, and sometimes we question whether what we do makes a difference. Bless our thoughts with new understanding and our deeds with renewed fulfillment, and help us spread your healing power across the lonely and forgotten places where your pilgrims stumble. Give us a hope to share, a love to impart, and a joy to uplift our neighbor, we pray. Amen.

The Twelfth Sunday after Pentecost

Meditation of Preparation

I take the road, not knowing
What will cross my path . . .
A chance? An invitation? A requirement?
Every journey has its daily pressures;
Every path provides a challenge and surprise!
Will the turn ahead offer an unexpected blessing
Or somehow change the story of my life?

Call to Consecration

Leader: We are busy wanderers in the maze of opportunities.

People: Pressed to succeed, we often stretch to please, to meet demands, and to survive.

Leader: Caught between expectations and beliefs, we are often driven into behaviors we dislike.

People: Please enter our misguided paths, and redirect us when we stray, Creator God.

Leader: Retrieve us when we wander aimlessly with meager wisdom, oppressed by harsh demands.

People: When we are bewildered and dismayed, save us from resignation and defeat.

Leader: Reorder disassembled worthy goals, reverse upended values, renew worn, well-appointed purposes.

People: Reshape our thoughts to fit your will, our eyes to see your way, our hearts to do your love, that we may leave this place walking a higher road, and in your grace!

Lead Scripture: Isaiah 25:6-9 and Mark 15:20-23

Sermon Meditation: "Unexpected Invitations"
We are creatures dulled by habit and preoccupation who notice little that is new or different in our day; every day provides surprising signals of God's action; a learned alertness to God's surprising daily revelation will increase our confidence and faith to follow God

Pastoral Prayer

Our daily fare has become such a routine, Lord, that we often go through the motions and forget to look closer at surprises and invitations in the path. We are so accustomed to the sameness that we've probably missed a new word from you, or a healing gesture to reverse the drudgery we're in. Meet us once again in the fixed furrows of our habits, and help us rise to new vistas and actions! Forgive us also for walking through your ever-renewed creation as if every day is the same, and as if you do not plan to surprise us with new invitations to abundant living. Our fear of change often prevents our awareness and response to what you have in store; nudge us again into the treasure of your ongoing activity in our midst and in our walk, we pray. Amen.

The Thirteenth Sunday after Pentecost

Meditation of Preparation

I eat the bread of worry and concern
And grope to hold the cup of life
Between my lips. I am an anxious pilgrim,
Trudging between safe places and shelters,
Seeking protection from the scorching sun.
I need the bread of hope, the cup
That will fulfill the deeper crevices inside
My withered life. Is there a trail ahead?

Call to Discovery and Grace

Leader: We are a needy and often poorly equipped people, Shepherd Friend!

People: We are poor in purpose, commitment, and care.

Leader: We are a rich people, Lord:

People: We are rich in grace, second chances, and clear tomorrows.

Leader: Erase our yesterdays, forgiving God, wherever they've been filled with hurt, despair, or selfishness.

People: Repeat our yesterdays, graceful God, whenever they were lived in care, in peaceful actions, and in service.

Leader: Increase, we pray, our capacity to learn from you, and love.

People: Increase also our willingness to trust, to give, and to risk loving, for the sake of good!

Leader: Enlarge our awareness of need and our resources to provide for others.

People: Strengthen our resolve to heal, our eagerness to serve, our openness to grow, that we may more fittingly become the people of your covenant!

Lead Scripture: Exodus 16:11-16 and John 6:25-27, 30-34

Sermon Meditation: "Filled, and Unfulfilled"
There are identified "foods" for the soul that have limited sustenance to offer us; God provides sometimes disguised resources for our spiritual strength; the Spirit of God can help us find the enduring "spiritual food" that lasts

Pastoral Prayer

Touch our dormant and unresponsive thoughts and actions, Master of the Way, and reverse the wasted steps and unimportant choices we entertain; heal our broken dreams and our vacant motions. Remove the preoccupations that plague our capacity to focus on your will and design for us. Stir within us imaginative and creative ways to care and live, and engage our capacity to do the good you want. Remove again our anxieties and distractions, heal our memories of distressing times and uncaring relationships. Remind us once again that you are with us in our struggles and capable of redeeming our times and blessing our efforts, please. For your sake and for ours, we pray. Amen.

The Fourteenth Sunday after Pentecost

Meditation of Preparation

The love of labor soon is lost
In frantic goals and driven hands;
Is there a pause that makes work glad?
Where is the rest that brings reward?
Reflection—that gives birth to focus?
Satisfaction—in brief contemplation?
When can I rest, for celebration?

Call to Renewal and Rest

Leader: O One who is not seen or touched, yet touches all who seek:

People: Incline your heart and ear and listen to us as we plead and seek your face.

Leader: We are willing slaves to well-known senses: we must touch and see, hear and taste, test and prove;

People: Yet you yourself are far beyond our scope and sense—close to us but not subject to control,

Leader: Accessible yet beyond our touch, available but not limited by our perceptions.

People: Seek us who seek you, and expand our range and grasp of who you are—and how you come into our life.

Leader: Forgive us the temptation to reduce you to our small, pale images; expand our sensitivity to hear you from a better dimension, to see you from a clearer point of view,

People: And to touch and be touched by you from a more informed imagination; help us who see to improve our sight; help us who hear to listen well;

Leader: Help us who reach to touch; who seek to find.

People: Grant us an awareness far beyond our senses, a power greater than our own, a love stronger than our fears, a hope above our narrow vision,

All: That we may follow long beyond our cautious faith, and find you as Creator, Redeemer, and Friend!

Lead Scripture: Exodus 33:18-23; 2 Corinthians 4:17-18; Hebrews 11:1-3

Sermon Meditation: "The Value of the Unseen"
We tend to place our faith in things that are visible and subject to our senses; some of the most important experiences in life are invisible;

the realm of truth, love, and faith are invisible realities of greatest substance

Pastoral Prayer

We have looked for you, and listened for you, all with our imperfect skills, Lord of life. Our fears and struggles often prevent clarity of sight and sound, and we now eagerly anticipate some message of hope and encouragement from you. We've lost perspective during the week, and we return to find the way you meant for us to take. Enable us to sense your presence beyond the limitations of our inadequate senses, we pray. Hear our inner pleas, even when words fail us; give us direction when confusion and doubt keep us away from you. Create new ways for us to think and act, and give us courage to follow by faith when we cannot see the road ahead or hear your voice. By your grace and mercy, we pray. Amen.

The Fifteenth Sunday after Pentecost

Meditation of Preparation

Dreams woo the child, bewilder youth,
And tease the full-grown soul!
Dreams also shape the serving heart
And lead the wandering mind.
Dreams are the stepping stones
That pave a path and point the way
To where I'll go, fulfilled, someday . . .

Call to Awareness and Joy

Leader: Guide us to dream a dream that lasts, Great Dreamer.

People: Teach us who seek to seek the things that matter.

Leader: Help us, O God of Joy, to choose fulfilling dreams; help us discern between fantasy and reality,

People: Falsehood and truth, authenticity and deception, what is empty and what is full of promise!

Leader: Sustain us also when our dreams are gone, or empty, to find new, rich, and hopeful dreams.

People: Dispel the selfish dream, the unworthy aspiration, and the timid search.

Leader: And thank you for the dreams that brought us to this day, with visions that inhabit our tomorrows and call us to abundant and fulfilling ways to live each day.

People: Dream on with us, O Spirit of all sacred dreams!

Lead Scripture: Genesis 37:3-8, 9-11 and Acts 2:17-18

Sermon Meditation: "Daydreaming and Dreaming"
The capacity to imagine and create thought is a powerful gift; dreaming and imagining are part of being in the image of God; God calls us through imagination, dreaming, and reflecting to participate in God's purpose for life itself

Pastoral Prayer

We come to dream with you, Spirit of Hope. We confess that some of our dreams have been selfish ambitions, and that we have often been driven by personal gain and little interest in others or your will. Return us again to the greater purposes you designed for us by placing us at the center of your desire and plans. Help us shed shallow and distracting goals and dreams; assist us to discard expectations and dreams that don't fit us. Sustain us when we harbor unfinished and difficult intentions, and comfort us when we must abandon dreams and hopes that are unattainable. Then, by your grace and mercy, lift us up to dream again, in richer ways, for better things, assisted by your creative presence and imagination. In your most holy name, we pray. Amen.

The Sixteenth Sunday after Pentecost

Meditation of Preparation

He walked into my life and pried open
My eyes, and then opened my heart:
Since then my hands have joined
My heart and sight—ready to care;
Reaching, to love! What else
Will this Man change in me—before he's done?

Call to Confession and Gratitude

Leader: We thank you, Creator God, for the privilege and challenge of worship.

People: We give you thanks for the constant reminder that we are family, and not alone;

Leader: That we share your purposes, not just our own; that we are the created, you the one who made and makes us!

People: Dispel the gloom of failed experiences, the pain of broken relationships, the loss of cherished plans.

Leader: Create before us tasks worthy of your gifts in us; provide for us people you want us to love and care for; shape in us purposes in keeping with your plans for us.

People: Thank you for imagination and insight, opportunity and talent, time and labor, which give us pleasure and fulfillment.

Leader: Renew our understanding of what you have for us to do in this world; open our senses to the invitations to causes and services in character with you.

People: Open our hearts to your measure of generosity and eagerness, so that we may become carriers of fulfillment and joy.

Leader: Touch our hands with your hands—pierced in love and serving, that our hands may carry compassion, mercy, and healing in this fractured world.

People: May we thus become your messengers of hope, transformation, and grace, because we have received the same ourselves!

Lead Scripture: Exodus 20:1-6 and John 2:13-17

Sermon Meditation: "Selective Service"
We have been called to lead a life of justice, mercy, and service; following Christ means doing his will and following his example; following Christ's will means getting involved in the care of his children

Pastoral Prayer

Meet us again, Agent of grace, more than halfway in our reunion. We've returned again almost empty handed from a week that has required its toll; we are worn down, we seek rest and shelter—we also seek sanity of purpose in a disconnected journey. Our best-made plans have gone astray in the rigors of scattered demands; our commitment to make a difference has dissolved in the face of opposition and apathy. Can you replenish spiritual depletion? Will your healing hands touch the frayed edges of our intentions and refurbish them? Forgive and free us, Lord, to serve you better, we pray. Amen.

The Seventeenth Sunday after Pentecost

Meditation of Preparation

I sing the song that fills my heart
With apathy or love,
Contempt or care; the words I write,
Inscribed for life, shape tunes
Of peace, concern, or strife. What is the song
Played—in my heart?

Call to Confession and Grace

Leader: We bring our broken hearts to you, Mender of Lives.

People: We have cared, tried hard, worked hard, and loved; and sometimes we've been wounded, by design or not.

Leader: Mend our brokenness, that we may care again; repair the damage caused by unfeeling gestures, betrayal, and casual deeds.

People: Rework the chords of compassion, drained and worn from causes too important to abandon and beliefs too significant to ignore.

Leader: Remind us of your faithful heart, broken itself in care for us and for all your children.

People: Retool our lives, that we may once again choose wisely, care deeply, and give to others with the same abandon with which you have gifted us!

Leader: Open our hearts to work in this your damaged world, doing your good, loving your way, helping the broken hearted on our path,

People: That we may join your healing of all souls, big and small, simple and strong, doing your loving will from day to day!

Lead Scripture: Jeremiah 31:31-33 and John 13:31-35

Sermon Meditation: "A New Commandment"

People committed to God share an internal transformation; faith in God generates a higher level of love and commitment; Christ challenges his followers to reproduce his love with everyone

Pastoral Prayer

We wish we had no fears, Lord—but we do:
We fear that our doubts are greater than our faith;
We sometimes fear that evil is stronger than good;
We fear that our apathy overcomes purpose and resolve;
We fear the unknown;
We are also anxious about much and secure about little;
We are anxious about the future and preoccupied more than at peace;

We are frequently also not obedient, and wonder if you can still forgive us.

Can you move us past our fears and our anxieties to greater trust and obedience?

Can you offer strength in the weak places and call us to increased determination?

Can you redouble our faith and strengthen us to a finer purpose?

Please do so, even as we wait and trust your redemptive work in us once more. . . .

Through Jesus Christ, our Friend, we pray.

The Eighteenth Sunday after Pentecost

Meditation of Preparation

I seek an absent God
Whose silence haunts my search. . . .
Am I alone? Is God not here?
What does the stillness say?
Is it a friend to faith? I cannot tell.
Where are you, who declared
You're here, and care?

Call to Awareness and Hope

Leader: My God, my God: Have you forsaken me? I cry by day but do not hear an answer, and at night but find no rest from my concern.

People: Yet you are the One Israel called holy, enthroned by our ancestors with praise!

Leader: In you our many generations have trusted, placed their hopes, and you delivered them.

People: They cried to you as we do and were saved from their plight; they trusted you and were not put to shame;

Leader: But we sometimes feel unimportant, less than human, often rejected and ignored by those to whom we turn for love.

People: We here commit our struggles and our hopes to you, dear God, believing that you will rescue us from our suspicions that we are on our own, that you don't care or cannot hear us.

Leader: It was you who nurtured us from birth, and have sustained us since, and have been our salvation.

People: Do not go far from us, we plead, for trouble seems so near, and no one can help as you can; lift us up, Provider God, and lead us by still waters to your peace-filled Presence! (Adapted from Psalms 22 and 23)

Lead Scripture: Psalm 22:1-11 and Acts 17:22-28

Sermon Meditation: "A Cry of Absence?"
Believers sometimes fear that God is no longer present or engaged in their lives; the perception of an absent Creator stirs bewilderment, doubt, frustration, and fear; God is still present in the silence and in the agony of searching, and also in the waiting for God

Pastoral Prayer

Praying is a strange and awkward exercise, O One who says you're listening. We utter words into the wind, and hope somehow that they rise up to you, somewhere far beyond us and yet close enough to hear! Knowing what to share, and what to say, is oftentimes bewildering; wondering if we're speaking to ourselves is sometimes a suspicion; and yet, in the deeper parts of our souls, we believe you are listening, and that you have not forgotten us, and that you care for us. Please listen to our confusion when no one else does. Please help us find some comfort in a selfish and competing world! Reaffirm parts of our faith that falter, redirect us to ways of hope, and help us share your reassurance and your strength with others, we pray. In Jesus' name, Amen.

The Nineteenth Sunday after Pentecost

Meditation of Preparation

So many words are hurled
Into the air—so many
Rules are made and not obeyed;
So many orders set and never kept.
How does commitment come to life?
How does a lifeless rule become a living tool?
When does the written part enter the heart?

Call to Worship and Awareness

Leader: It's easy to utter quick words, spout meaningless phrases, even utter commitments, Faithful One.

People: But it's so much harder to mean what we say and to keep covenants we've expressed!

Leader: Save us from vain repetitions and empty promises, dear God.

People: We want to be as good as our word; we wish to be reliable followers, responsible servants, worthy believers;

Leader: Yet we often forget what we said we would do, what we declared we would become, what we vowed we would learn.

People: Our words can float, too easily, from our lips, and too soon disappear in the busyness of secondhand pursuits and habits.

Leader: Vain repetitions need to be replaced with tangible actions and behaviors,

People: So challenge us, dear God, to make sacred promises as you do, and to honor them, adding resolve and eager determination!

Lead Scripture: Deuteronomy 4:5-9 and Mark 7:1-7

Sermon Meditation: "Speaking from the Heart"

Some pilgrims know the words of faith but do not practice God's care and love; true understanding of God's love transforms the heart and creates action; transformed believers evidence a new compassion and attitude toward others and toward their own mission in the world

Pastoral Prayer

We use so many words, and often say so little! Creator God, you listen patiently to things we say, whether deep or shallow, and you grace us when most of our vocabulary is about ourselves. We confess that we spend much time preoccupied, and share our worries and our fears long before we ask to serve your cause. Thank you for caring for our small concerns, and walking with us through our troubles, and staying by when we fail, or fall. Teach us again how to make vows that last, and help us follow you responsibly and maintain our faith at every turn. We pray, and ask it in your name. Amen.

The Twentieth Sunday after Pentecost (Life Stewardship Sunday)

Meditation of Preparation

I came into this world
A fragile, unprotected child, and made it
Through the day because of loving arms
And love; I walk, now, on my own,
Strong, able, and secure, and stretch a helping hand
To someone else, who places a small hand in mine
And knows I'll also care because my heart is glad!

Responsive Child, Parent, Church Dedication

Leader: We celebrate with parents here the miracle and gift of a child!

Parents: We share our joy with the family of God, who gives us strength and nurture as we provide for this child!

Leader: Will you remember, parents, that you are trusted with this child, made in God's image and shared with you as a tender blessing and hope?

Parents: We receive this child as a miracle of creation, a dear challenge and affirmation, a sure promise, and a sacred trust.

Leader: Will you promise, by God's grace and wisdom, to teach your child about God's love, and nurture and provide this little one with faith and love?

Parents: With God's grace and wisdom, we do so promise.

Leader: Will you, the family of God, accept your call to nurture and to guide, to encourage and sustain, to model and to bless each child, each parent, here before you?

Congregation: We will. We have been called to support and to teach, to love and to guide, to lead and to provide, to offer our strength and faith to these children, born into God's family and received by these parents we love.

All: May God's Spirit give us wisdom to bring up these children in their own sacred purpose, and may we follow God's will for their nurture with thanksgiving and joy!

Lead Scripture: Psalm 112:5-9 and Acts 2:43-47

Sermon Meditation: "Glad Hearts"
God has shared the joy of generosity as one of the secrets of being made in God's image; being at peace with one's needs and wanting to share with others is a key to finding generosity; the greatest joy is found in the experience of giving out of gratitude for what we have received

Pastoral Prayer

Dear God, you have called us as a nurturing Creator to form family and sustain each other in your manner and image. We here and now renew our covenants of care: with you, as the Author of life and purpose, and with one another, as brother and sister in a community of faith you've brought together! Remind us as we gather together today of other sheep in your flock, some of whom feel isolated and forgotten and need to know that they, too, belong to you, and to us as God's family. Help us seek those who are wounded and heavy laden and offer them the rest and peace that comes from you. Guide us also to bring our own burdens to you, that we may trust you with our cares. Bless also all assembled here who care for others, that they may know your wisdom and strength, and teach us what it means to live as the family of God in this time and place. In the name of our brother, Jesus Christ, we pray. Amen.

The Twenty-first Sunday after Pentecost

Meditation of Preparation

Here I am again, Lord: Tired
Of the journey, hoping for something
I've not found. I've taken the long path,
The hard path, the wrong path—
And even wondered if there was a path!
Meet me, please, somewhere in the middle
Of a clearing, and show me where to step, so I can follow!

Call to Awareness and Purpose

Leader: We've come into a crowded room with doubts and expectations, Giver of Life.

People: We bring our doubts because our doubts and questions belong in worship;

Leader: Our expectations also prompt us to inquire and search.

People: We gather to remember that you're really there, and here, that you care about what happens to us, about what we're doing in the world you made.

Leader: Remind us that it's not our will and way that saves the world, but yours.

People: Remind us also that you care about our agony, our confusion, our doubts, and that you bring us peace of mind, recovery of soul, and purpose, once lost!

Leader: Help us sense your presence in a senseless week, your care in careless places, your love in loveless moments.

People: Help us embrace our doubts as doors to faith, our fears as paths to courage, our restlessness as a road to peace of mind.

Leader: Erase pretense, dispel anxiety, encourage faith, forgive excessive caution, bless inquiry!

People: Foster hope and love, that we may touch the Holy once again, find grace, rise up in newness, and walk in your light!

Lead Scripture: Proverbs 2:3-6 and Mark 7:31-37

Sermon Meditation: "Worship as Replenishment"
We come each week to the worship hour fatigued and needy; our burdens are lifted as we confess our frailty and find grace, and as our faith is renewed; we return to a week of labor replenished and refreshed by the grace and care of God

Pastoral Prayer

We're not always sure of what to say or ask for in our prayers, dear God. The jumble of thoughts and mixed emotions distracts us enough that we rarely can focus on things that matter. Help us set aside our preoccupations, we pray, so that we may find some peace of mind and heart. Sustain us in places where we are troubled, and add perspective to our fears and questions. Elevate our search for truth and justice, and keep us grounded in the faith that has been a sure companion from early days. Guide us also to find places of service and care where we may multiply your love in this imperfect and often selfish existence. In your most holy name we ask and pray. Amen.

The Twenty-second Sunday after Pentecost

Meditation of Preparation

I've been pressed and challenged,
Pushed and pressured, badgered and ignored;
Living by surprise and burden, I've also
Been invited to form courage
In this wilderness of emptiness and strife.
I can also give myself to worthy matters,
Conquer obstacles, overcome adversity,
Set a higher standard. How will I respond?

Call to Commitment and Courage

Leader: We gather at your generous altar, both to give and to receive, dear Maker.

People: You gave birth to everything, including us, and called it "good"!

Leader: Give birth again to all that's possible and good in us.

People: Shape us to serve and love in ways that reflect your nature and will, we pray.

Leader: Remove from our hearts all inclination to suspicion, apathy, jealousy, and hatred.

People: Move through the chaos of our still unformed priorities, and mold our minds toward concern, compassion, care, and love for neighbor, and for your designs.

Leader: Free us from the darkness of fear and preconception; cause light to reveal paths of understanding and generosity.

People: Illumine our starved attitudes; make us ambassadors of hope in helpless places; a ray of light to all who've lost their way;

Leader: A word of grace to all who feel condemned; a sign of love to all who fear abandonment.

People: Take loaves and fishes from our trembling hands, and multiply your care and blessing with them, that we ourselves may marvel at the miracle you make with meager gifts!

Lead Scripture: 1 Kings 19:9-16 and Matthew 15:32-37

Sermon Meditation: "What the World Needs Now"
We are pilgrims seeking purpose and meaning in our daily path; God reminds us that discipleship involves courage, faith, and commitment to superior values; when we embrace the gifts of grace, courage, and highest values, we hold what people everywhere need the most

Pastoral Prayer

Dear One who feeds us when we hunger and quenches our thirst when we wither: walk again into our crowded steps and sustain us, please. The road we share is arduous and demanding, and our spirits flag and fail. Sometimes the requirements of a given week press us down and empty us of resources and options. We return unfilled to you again, believing that you can replenish empty hands and discouraged hearts. Fill us with hope and focus, that we ourselves may deliver joy and purpose, and multiply your enduring peace and satisfying purpose. We pray all this in the name and way of Jesus Christ, Friend and Savior to forgotten and fainting servants. Amen.

The Twenty-third Sunday after Pentecost (Christ the King Sunday, Thanksgiving Week)

Meditation of Preparation

Somehow he saw: I'd kept my withered hand
Away from public stares
And helpless gestures of reserved compassion.
He also knew I owned a withered heart,
Untouched by love, or care, unchanged by any hope—

Until he came, and found me
In a crowd of withered souls . . . . My hand,
And heart, will never be the same. Will yours?

Call to Gladness and Gratitude

Leader: We've brought all the strange assortment of emotions for your care, O Lord:

People: Our sadness over wars that do not end, our fear for people in peril, our helplessness to settle our differences,

Leader: Our frustration with evil, our pain over injustice and selfishness.

People: But you have shown us that you can help us win even the wars within us, and that you can conquer our frailty and transform us into instruments of healing and redemption.

Leader: We give you thanks for the peace you bring in the face of turmoil and distress; for the sound of joy that fills our days when we see love prevail, service multiplied, and blessings shared!

People: With gratitude we acknowledge that creation itself continues to bloom each day with the majesty of the color and aroma you provide;

Leader: Mountain and valley, tree and flower, spring waters and the music of birds herald your continued care!

People: Renew us also, that we may blossom in service and compassion every day and act as eager carriers of your re-forming hope and elevated dreams!

Lead Scripture: Psalm 107:1-9; Mark 3:1-5; Philippians 4:4-8

Sermon Meditation: "Finding Gratitude"

We take many wonderful things we experience for granted; God has provided many joys for us out of an abundance of love and generosity; a rich and meaningful response to God's generosity is an ongoing attitude of gratitude

Pastoral Prayer

There is so much we take for granted, Maker of Life. We traipse daily into your amazing garden, filled with color and grace—as if we deserve to live in it! We assume that the diversity of the seasons and the variety of our opportunities are ours to enjoy, but we rarely pause to say we're grateful for the One who made it all, and offers it to us! Thank you also for the extraordinary gift of being made in your image, so that we can dream, and care, and love, create and shape, express compassion, and belong! Inspire us to remember that what we have is not just for us to possess but a gift and means to bless and share joy and fulfillment with others in our human journey. Thank you, dear generous Friend, for all you've given us and all we can pass on! Amen.

YEAR TWO

The Season of Advent

The First Sunday of Advent

Meditation of Preparation

I travel by so many signs
And miss the message,
Busied by my wandering mind.
Thanks to my preoccupation,
Have I missed a bush still burning?
Missed a pillar, fire by night?
And have I just gone by a stable—
Without seeing what's inside?

Call to Awareness and Perspective

Leader: We still seek you in old forms, familiar places, dated language, and worn trappings, Holy One.

People: Open our eyes to see what we have missed before, our ears to hear what we've not heard, and our faith to still notice signs of your appearance!

Leader: You've chosen to surprise us once by clothing yourself as a child, tiptoeing into a stable, snuggling up to a peasant family, and arriving in the cover of darkness;

People: Surprise us once again, we plead, for we no longer seem to expect you anymore . . . .

Leader: Help us who still seek signs of your appearance to notice signs already given us;

People: Help us, so unprepared, to be prepared for you, and watch for you with new anticipation;

Leader: In unexpected ways, at unexpected moments, walk again into our hearts and minds;

People: Stir up forgotten promptings, gentle invitations, and the pleasure of a sacred presence quietly in our midst!

Lead Scripture: 1 Kings 19:8-13 and Luke 21:25-31

Sermon Meditation: "Still Looking for a Sign?"
We are pilgrims regularly seeking evidence of God's presence in our life; God often uses subtle and unpretentious means to declare God's presence and care; the simple and humble birth of Jesus Christ in a small town to a peasant family was God's quiet, unpretentious, and greatest declaration of care for us

Pastoral Prayer

We live in a distracting and suspicious time, dear Child of Hope. Our journey is littered with deceptive signs and empty invitations. We've come into your house of worship seeking reliable signs of encouragement and hope; left to our own designs, life is still vacant and void! We need your promptings to overcome our faltering steps and inadequate living. We need our faith rebirthed, our focus reset, our values reformed; please enter our confusion and preoccupation, and give birth to the way of life you envisioned when you brought forth this world. Remake us in your image, saving child, that we may ourselves be born again, re-find newness of purpose, and follow! Through Christ, our hope, we pray. Amen.

The Second Sunday of Advent

Meditation of Preparation

I brought my restlessness
Into the solitude inside the room;
The storm I felt was deep within,

The struggle there I try to hide . . . .
Am I the only one who doubts?
Does no one else inquire, or wonder?
Just then awakened by the sound
Of someone gently being born,
I felt a quietness inside.
Was God—delivering a child?

Call to Confession and Peace

Leader: We've gathered again as pilgrims seeking peace and perspective for the divided world in which we live, Prince of Peace.

People: We are sometimes bewildered, sometimes troubled, sometimes absolutely lost!

Leader: We expect too much, and expect too little: we want a world that's fair, comfortable, and secure.

People: We expect you to protect us from all harm, provide our every whim, bring us harmony, and treat us as the favorite child in your family.

Leader: We also expect too much of ourselves, of our families, of our labors.

People: We need to find a peace that overpowers the anger and alienation all around us; we also seek an inner peace for troubling thoughts and self-devaluation.

Leader: Heal us of the excessive self-judgment that oppresses us, the weight of unforgiveness that lingers, the burden of unnecessary self-condemnation;

People: Make us also ambassadors of reconciliation and harmony, that we may heal broken and wounded relationships,

Leader: And serve as instruments of peace and hope in a turbulent and alienated world.

People: Come, Messenger of peace and friend to the forgotten, and save us from our fears and doubts!

Lead Scripture: Isaiah 9:6-7 and Luke 1:76-79

Sermon Meditation: "Peace—on Earth?"

We are residents of a stressful and disturbing world; God is the author and giver of enduring peace and serenity; Christ was born into our strained lives to offer us a lasting peace

Pastoral Prayer

O One who came to bring us deeper peace and hope, can you restore a sense of calm to our beleaguered and stressed lives? We struggle daily with schedules and requirements that oppress us; we submit to pressures that reduce our joy and tranquility. We've come into your sanctuary eager to find solace from the strain of daily worries and concerns. You were the one who called us into being and purposed an abundant quality of life: Restore us, then, to your designs and plans, and deliver us from petty requirements and unattainable expectations. Cause us once again to embrace the true peace that comes from shaping our hopes to your grace-filled values. Raise our sight to recognize your gentle presence in our journey, sustain us in the hard places, and celebrate with us in our successes, we pray. In your most holy name, we ask. Amen.

The Third Sunday of Advent

Meditation of Preparation

The darkness often seems
To muscle out the dawn.
The bad, no doubt, also
May trump the good!
But, then, in unimpressive ways,
The gift of healing may appear.
Is Bethlehem nearby? Is just
A peasant child, too small?
Or can joy overcome despair—
In smallest sizes, in uncharted places?

Call to Celebration

Leader: Our lives confess our daily need of you, Small Child of Bethlehem.

People: Stressed by demands, challenged by unyielding expectations, and pressed by the tyranny of our own requirements,

Leader: We have often lost sight of what is most important, most helpful, most gratifying.

People: Your gift of joy eludes us, for we are distracted by distressing sorrows.

Leader: Show us again the road to inner happiness, paved with caring purposes, unselfish deeds, in concert with your will and way!

People: Heal our propensity to seek first our own comfort, so that we may be grasped by the fulfillment and serenity that comes in serving others.

Leader: Call us again to the stable of generous living, the manger of unqualified giving, and to its secret of abundant inner joy,

All: That we may kneel and worship your unfailing revelation, rise as carriers of an exultant gladness to an injured and divided world, and call all people to the healing Presence in the stable!

Lead Scripture: Isaiah 2:1-5 and Romans 13:8-12

Sermon Meditation: "From Darkness to Dawn"
We are creatures who struggle with darkness, confusion, and cluelessness; Christ came into our world to give clarity and light to our darkness; believers who follow Christ find clarity of purpose, direction, and light for the journey

Pastoral Prayer

Giver of all good gifts, we stand in line this season hoping to receive a gift from you. Are we late in asking? Are you still a willing giver? Do we ask for what we cannot have? Reassure us, please, that you have more to offer than we hold in our hands or hearts! Our cups are half empty and needing to be filled with everlasting hope; our hands seek vital gestures that can bless while being blessed; our thoughts need higher aspirations than we've settled for; and our souls need mending from the sadness and the sorrow still contained inside. Cause us again to delight in your purposes and to be transformed by the radiance of your gracious, forgiving smile, we pray—in the name of the Christ child, our Savior and our deepest joy! Amen.

The Fourth Sunday of Advent

Meditation of Preparation

Alone, but not by choice,
My empty, solitary frame
Awaits beyond the empty promises
That never fill the void . . . .
Will hope, again, betray me? Will peace deceive me?
Is this another journey by myself?
Or—is the one who made me
Willing to walk beside me
And be born in my travail?

Call to Affirmation and Wonder

Leader: We want to trust you and follow, but we have questions, much doubt, and many competing allegiances, Child of Bethlehem.

People: Help us sort through the many voices that confuse us, that we may recognize your voice of purpose and commitment.

Leader: We are easily distracted and dismayed; our worship is at times a set of empty gestures and vain repetitions.

People: Protect us from shallow living and behaviors so routine that love is but a distant thought;

Leader: Relieve us of pretense and posture, and rekindle in us a greater understanding of the meaning of your love in Bethlehem.

People: Step gently into our dreams and hearts, and renew our capacity to care, our willingness to love, and our openness to fathom that you love us—

Leader: And that you love us enough to enter this often cold and uncaring world as a small child, to give us a face to recognize your warming presence and invisible embrace.

People: Touch us with such generous grace that we may leave this place believing once again that we are lovable, that you believe in us, and that you've come to bridge the distance we have felt from God!

Lead Scripture: Isaiah 7:13-14 and Matthew 1:22-23

Sermon Meditation: "God with Us?"
The often misunderstood and unknown Creator and Sustainer of life has tried to reach us with love—in history, patriarchs, judges, and prophets; God next decided to come in human form to give us a face as Emmanuel; Christ born in Bethlehem is God's presence in a human life that we can understand and follow

Pastoral Prayer

"Love" is an easy word to say, and easily misunderstood, Good Maker. You know our secret: we do not really love ourselves. We strive to believe that you can love us, too, for we know our inadequacies and flaws. If you listen to our thoughts, you know how much we question, how much we fear, how inconsistent we are. Can you forgive us for how we hesitate to follow, how often we don't care, and how soon we give up? Can you transform the suspicion that we harbor—that the stable was empty, that there was no star to follow, and that you really no longer care? Please enter our anxieties and lower their power; touch our fears and reduce them to useful inquiries; scatter and dispel our doubts; raise our sight to see the light you bring into our darkness, the strength you offer to our weakness, and the faithfulness you add to our frailty. Help us recover confidence in your love for us and in our hope for tomorrow, we pray—through Christ, who risked himself to bring us face to face with you. Amen.

The First Sunday after Christmas

Meditation of Preparation

The party's over, all
The guests have gone,
And the silence in the room
Reflects my quiet mood.
I'm in a crowd, but by myself,
Remembering what I've left
Unfinished and abandoned for the year . . . .
Is there another start?
A new beginning?

Call to Reflection and Purpose

Leader: We've come to return an unfinished year to you, Creator God.

People: We have unfinished deeds, incomplete promises, untried dreams in our hands.

Leader: We need grace for promises to you and to ourselves we did not or could not keep.

People: We also come to ask that you assist us to shape a new year filled with hope, fidelity to promises made, and strength to reach our potential!

Leader: Teach us to choose our commitments and plans carefully, and help us make more worthy promises.

People: Encourage us to set aside the dreams that no longer fit us, and help us dream new dreams that challenge us to use our gifts as you intended, to follow your will and purposes for us.

Leader: Sustain us when we must learn to live between dreams, and grant us the patience to trust you as we wait for our next vision with you.

People: Today we still look back to a year that has challenged and stretched us: we are not the same for having walked this year with you.

Leader: Teach us to hear new songs you have for us, that we may sing new melodies, embrace a year of promise, and take hold of faith in brand new ways!

People: Finish in us the transformation you've begun within us, that we may rise to new levels of commitment and service in the year ahead, we pray.

Lead Scripture: Isaiah 61:11–62:2 and 1 Corinthians 2:9-10

Sermon Meditation: "A New Name and a New Song?"
Certain "beginnings" give us a chance to look back—and look forward—in life; careful reflection will identify unfinished projects, promises, and plans; God calls us by grace to leave some things undone, reaffirm others, and commit to new things

Pastoral Prayer

The end of the year brings us to the edge of what we can see and know, dear God. We give you thanks for every experience that has enlarged our faith, every challenge that has increased our courage to follow, and every relationship you've sent our way that has touched and blessed us in this year that is ending! As we close a chapter and open another one, help us to hear your voice and follow your lead. There are things we must leave behind and new things we must take hold of; give us wisdom to know the difference, and sustain us as we cross into a new, uncharted territory. Prepare a path, that we may be faithful to follow; prepare our hearts, that we may learn new ways to love and care; and guide us past any selfish ambitions, that we may engage our best in serving you and in growing in favor with your will, we pray. Amen.

The Season of Epiphany

Epiphany Sunday

Meditation of Preparation

He comes we know not when
And bids us often wait;
Still, born in unexpected ways,
He may surprise us.
Sometimes in the shadows, sometimes
In plain sight, suddenly
We catch a glimpse of him, and know
We've seen—the light!

Call to Alertness and Surprise

Leader: Though we walk through the valley,

People: Yes, through, not around the valley of the shadows, and death:

Leader: You are with us!

People: Though we stumble,

Leader: You will keep us;

People: Though the waters swell and threaten, still you will command the waters.

Leader: Part the waters so they will not overwhelm us,

People: And bring us safely to the other side!

Leader: You, O God, will also part the heavens, come to join us,

People: Find us, save us, keep us, till we join you—on the other side!

Lead Scripture: Isaiah 42:5-9 and Matthew 3:13-17

Sermon Meditation: "Surprised by God?"

The Almighty appears sometimes in moments unexpected, in most troubled times; God knows that during stress and challenge our faith is also challenged; our Shepherd God gently leads us from fear and inadequacy to comfort and peace in human trials

Pastoral Prayer

Too often we measure our next day by the dullness of our routine, Creator Friend. We rise, and run, and sit, and work, and sometimes dream and wonder—but often perceive our days as just a repetitive circle of sameness. Even our spiritual journey has a flavor of the expected and the altogether old. Can you still surprise us with a newer vision of ourselves? Can you stir our minds and hearts to imagine ourselves in new ways, and guide us to a new sense of your presence in our daily lives? Please help us reduce the distractions that prevent us from seeing the burning bush, pillar of fire, or guiding star you have provided for us. Teach us to anticipate each day as a spiritual adventure, each challenge as an invitation to wrestle a blessing from a roadblock on the road. Give us insight to see the world as Christ himself did, and every turn of the road as another conversation with your Spirit. In the name of your greatest surprise to us, Jesus the Christ, we pray. Amen.

The First Sunday after Epiphany

Meditation of Preparation

Can I take a new path
On a traveled road?
Is it possible to sing a new song
With an old tune?

Can a mind trained to repeat itself
Think a different way?
Can a heart accustomed
To known emotions
Experience something new?

Call to Affirmation and Discovery

Leader: We hold old memories of worship moments experienced long ago, with emotions and decisions we made then.

People: We come to celebrate the memory of those moments, and to add new ones

Leader: That will strengthen and add deeper faith to truths already held.

People: Find us again, dear God, even in the maneuvers we use to hide from you;

Leader: Touch dormant skills, and quicken faith and hope grown brittle from inattention!

People: Beckon us with the mystery of a new song, sung to a better chord;

Leader: Or in a prayer, expressed by stirring words and coming from the heart.

People: Save us, who have ceased to seek, from boredom and inertia;

Leader: Help us who falter to gain steadiness and comfort by your care;

People: Baptize and immerse us daily by the Spirit's presence;

Leader: And raise us up to follow, hope anew, and grow in grace!

Lead Scripture: Isaiah 42:9-12 and Matthew 3:11

Sermon Meditation: "New Things"
We are creatures of old habits that give us comfort—even in our faith; God always wants to add new dimensions to our faith and joy;

trusting God with new dimensions of faith and service brings spiritual vitality and energizing anticipation to our journey

Pastoral Prayer

We need the Spirit's breath today to whisper new dimensions and new dreams into our untrained hearing, Master Planner. We've tried old ways of thinking, old habits, and old songs along the way, and we need new stanzas and new music for a brand new road! Sometimes we fear that nothing on this road will ever change, that we will muddle through the same tried behaviors and narrow views again; we need to know that you have untried plans for us, that you are walking with us into unknown vistas that will enlarge our hopes and brighten our tomorrows. We count already on your unfailing presence. Please remind us that you are always making new things, tapping new skills, shaping new dreams for us, and inviting us into a future full of grace and crisp opportunities for growth and joy. Guide us to new heights! In the name of the One who always multiplies our daily bread, we pray. Amen.

The Second Sunday after Epiphany

Meditation of Preparation

How long we live before we find
The things most apt to give us joy!
The secret truths that give life "soul,"
Disguised, appear at every turn . . .
Purpose in service, labor as gift,
Rich promises fulfilled.
How strange to seek
For things already in my grasp!

Call to Care and Dedication

Leader: Are we like shepherds, bored with the routine of the
       evening, missing the music in the air?

People: Have we been distracted by the glitter and the labor, and missed the star?

Leader: Do we come bearing gifts, while never having found the greatest Gift ourselves?

People: Can we see the light at the end of the darkness that always surrounds us?

Leader: Receive our plea, generous Giver, that we may still believe the wonderful truth that you have chosen to live here in our fragile quarters.

People: Please remain with us at least until we've learned to love and not hate, to build and not destroy, to embrace and not ignore, to heal and not wound!

Leader: Come again, Emmanuel, ransom and release Israel, and release us also to do your love in places and with people needing it most, until you once again appear.

People: Touch and transform our waiting hearts and hopes, we pray, dear Friend!

Lead Scripture: Isaiah 7:10-17 and Mark 1:4-8

Sermon Meditation: "Preparing Our Hearts"
As constant seekers, we look for answers to the greatest satisfaction in life; too often bored with the familiar, we may devalue truth and faith already in our grasp; God invites us regularly to reflect and review insights and gifts already shared with us, for our benefit and for a deeper understanding

Pastoral Prayer

As another year unfolds, dear Maker, help us retain the focus of our promises and hopes. We want so much to do better, to live joy-filled lives, to honor your plans for us, yet we are aware of how inconsistent and uneven is our discipline, and how easily we fall into discouragement and carelessness. Keep working in our minds, to feed good dreams and worthy aspirations; keep stirring our hearts, to will and focus on service and healing; keep walking ahead of us, to sustain us in the rough spots; keep believing in us, even when we fail to believe in ourselves. Teach us to trust you with our troubles and our concerns, that they may not become worries that impede our path in this still new year; and lead us beside quiet waters, to your higher purposes and our fulfillment in them. In the name of the one who dared to come into our struggles and redeem us, Jesus Christ, we pray. Amen.

The Third Sunday after Epiphany

Meditation of Preparation

The search is still pursued
Although the seeker falters;
The missing factor
Haunts the failing hunter,
Who despairs and slowly
Gives up hope . . .
Is life played out? Is there
No more? What is the remedy
For an always restless soul?

Call to Confession and Grace

Leader: Here we are again, Engaging God, worn down from the daily pressures of unyielding schedules.

People: We seek your call to Sabbath, knowing that we have spent much energy in matters far removed from your concern.

Leader: Our resources are depleted on secondary goals, yet you have found us and sustained us every day.

People: Our energy is often consumed on things that bring little reward, and we return unfulfilled, seeking your wisdom.

Leader: Retool our minds to think in ways that follow your lead, and in choices that bring your will to bear upon a struggling world.

People: Reset our hearts to purposes that flower with meaning and care.

Leader: Renew our enthusiasm for life as you designed it, and our eagerness for justice and mercy.

People: Rekindle proper dreams, overloaded with our own ambitions; remake our journey, weighed down by heavy burdens.

Leader: Refresh our hopes, that we may blossom once again and flourish, like your creation—that we may multiply the blooming of your love!

Lead Scripture: Isaiah 62:1-4a and John 2:1-10

Sermon Meditation: "New Wine for Worn Lives"
God has designed renewal and replenishment in all creation; we regularly wear down from the burdens and challenges we carry; God in Christ has invited us in worship and daily pauses to recover strength and perspective, to find renewal of purpose and joy

Pastoral Prayer

Our cups return to you as empty vessels, seeking new wine and strength, dear Keeper of the vineyard. Our toil is great, our energy at times exhausted, and our need is for renewal—for service and focus. We need to find more joy in daily labor; we also need to find grace at the end of the day. We judge ourselves too harshly, and press beyond our skills and capacities; help us find boundaries to our worries, to our expectations, and to our disillusionment. Increase our capacity to love ourselves, our neighbor, and our labor. Transform weary efforts into opportunities for celebration and gratitude, even as we thank you for remaining with us when our spirits flag. We pray in the name and nature of the Christ Child, our Friend, Jesus Christ. Amen.

The Fourth Sunday after Epiphany

Meditation of Preparation

Engaged at first, I state my hopes
And dreams; then, turning to the task
Of making them come true, I falter,
Flinch, and fail. Why?
Why do I scuttle dreams before they sail?
Why do I quit on promises
Before they flourish? Is there a secret
Known only to a few?

Call to Awareness and Grace

Leader: We are a people of much promise, Creator God!

People: We are also a people of interrupted dreams, unrealized potential.

Leader: Help us today to recognize in ourselves potential we can find in a new year: untapped, unspent, and fresh with possibility.

People: Assist us to see ourselves through your eyes, that we may gaze at the unexplored dreams and hopes for which we have been formed.

Leader: Guide us to see our limitations as invitations to depend on you.

People: Enable us to uncover the untold potential dormant in us, yearning to be realized.

Leader: Remove the obstacles to a clear vision of ourselves as children of hope and promise.

People: Enrich our imagination for skills unused, good untried, experiences waiting to bless us,

Leader: That we may live on the edge of discovery, surprise, and fulfillment, in your name.

People: Create in us a pure heart, O God, and renew a steadfast spirit within us; restore to us the joy of salvation, and grant us a peace that sustains us!

Lead Scripture: Isaiah 42:5-7 and Luke 3:21-22

Sermon Meditation: "Taking Yourself Seriously"
We have been equipped by God to ask important questions about meaning, focus, and purpose in life; we settle often for superficial questions, ask too few questions, scuttle our potential, and interrupt our spiritual development; God calls us to take ourselves seriously, ask questions that will help us reach our potential, and spend time on responses that fit God's will for us

Pastoral Prayer

O God of many gifts and multiple invitations, allow us, please, to catch a glimpse of all the possibilities we miss because of our narrowed vision! Expand our vistas to consider challenges we've never tried, care we've never offered, service we've never extended. Teach us to come to the edge of everything we believe, and to reach forth in faith to learn and grow as we have never grown before. Remove the boredom and apathy that infect our willingness to follow. Renew our interest and affection for a deeper spiritual path, and call us to the center of your will and grace, we pray, that we may live the more abundant life in the name of the One who loved us enough to send us the Christ Child. Amen.

The Fifth Sunday after Epiphany

Meditation of Preparation

Unwelcome guest, and close
At hand, affliction comes
Announced, or not, and stuns
My fragile, once undaunted faith . . .
And what may happen to a soul
Assaulted, unprepared, and frail?

Either the loss of fragile truths,
Or greater strength
Born under pain!

Summons to Awareness and Grace

Leader: Receive us again, Maker of the Way, as wandering pilgrims on the road;

People: Renew our bodies, worn from worthy and unworthy pursuits;

Leader: Renew our minds, worn by distraction, worry, and concern;

People: Renew our spirits, tired from labor, leisure without purpose, and self-serving causes.

Leader: Teach us again the higher wisdom that will inform our choices;

People: Show us again the higher vision, which can bless our journey;

Leader: Give us again the higher Presence that rekindles joy and peace;

People: Stir the dying embers of a faith, that light and warmth may once again preside!

All: That we may run again and not grow weary; walk with you and not grow faint. Renew our strength and keep our sacred vows!

Lead Scripture: Hosea 11:1-4 and 2 Corinthians 4:7-16

Sermon Meditation: "Facing Afflictions"

Life interrupts designs and plans with injury, traumatic surprises, difficult afflictions; visitations with injury, injustice, and misery create challenges to faith and hope; the God of healing and hope works with us in the midst of injury and affliction to sustain and comfort us

Pastoral Prayer

We are a fortunate people, Lord of Many Cares: we have our daily bread, a place to rest our head, and a community of friends. Yet we are also sometimes afflicted, physically, emotionally, spiritually; we struggle to adjust to changes in our lives, and too soon we become discouraged in the fray of loss. Help us overcome our despondency over concerns we cannot change. Strengthen our courage and patience in the midst of pain or sorrow. Sustain us when our options are narrow and our perspectives small. Call us to a faith that will endure even in the valleys of life, and where there is darkness, equip us with determination born of commitment and endurance in the face of obstacles. Grant us the presence that brings peace to us in troubling days, and hope even when we face our limitations, we pray. Through Christ, who knows our struggles and conquers all defeats! Amen.

The Sixth Sunday after Epiphany

Meditation of Preparation

So many words, so little
Said, so little meant.
So many hopes, so many plans,
Such empty hands.
What does it mean to care
Enough, to really love?
And what's the chance
For such a gift?

Call to Worship and Care

Leader: Maker of dawning days, stunning miracles, and lavish invitations:

People: We, your children, gather around your altar, wearing hopeful faces, carrying heavy burdens, seeking illumination and presence.

Leader: The week has drawn our energy and effort, used up our resources, challenged our skills,

People: So we return unfilled to the Source of fulfillment, knowing that you are the sustainer of good dreams, the creator of hope, the giver of strength!

Leader: Fill our lives with newfound zest, fresh purpose, eager longings.

People: Restore tender aspirations, sometimes fragile hearts, and weakened hands.

Leader: Renew body, mind, soul, and spirit; return priority and purpose to their proper place.

People: Lift us up, to see your face in the horizon, gain confidence on our path, peace in our journey, and your welcome power in our daily labor!

Lead Scripture: Deuteronomy 30:19-20 and 1 Corinthians 13:1-7

Sermon Meditation: "Doing the Four-Letter Word"
We search each day for what will satisfy our basic needs; we are all designed by God to receive and offer relationship and love; Christ has come to show us the depth of God's love for us and how to actually love one another

Pastoral Prayer

Our words and actions have often lost their meaning, Maker God. We speak of love too easily, and practice it too little. We've returned to you for another focused lesson on the content of the word, listening for fidelity, care beyond ourselves, commitment and responsibility, and thoughtful affection. Teach us, then, first to love ourselves more properly, with a gentle touch of grace; then to love others, not so much because of who they are but because of who we are and what we believe. And help us also to learn how to love you, who patiently surrounds us with sustenance and care, joy and peace, and every good hope. Help us heal from the wounds of inadequate care and lack of love from others, and give us a measure of forgiveness to extend to those who know not how to love—that we may reflect your highest image in relationships. We pray as believers who want to multiply the love you brought into our lives, in Jesus Christ. Amen.

The Season of Lent

The First Sunday of Lent

Meditation of Preparation

I can be as much
Or as little as I choose to be:
I can choose to be a burden,
Live as a liability,
Walk a fruitless path.
I can also choose
To make a difference, plan
To leave a blessing
Everywhere. I can be
Whatever—if I will!

Call to Confession and Faith

One: What have we come to acknowledge?

Many: We've come to affirm that God's character is superior to ours:

One: With God there are no games, no manipulation, no mixed motives, no easy concessions,

Many: No short-term gratification; none of the confusion that often assails us.

One: Do we stray from being honest in this place? Do we struggle with stating our doubts and frustrations, and avoid sharing our fears and concerns, keeping our burdens to ourselves?

One: Sometimes we are so controlled by our own needs that we cannot see beyond ourselves.

Many: Preoccupation and anxiety keep us from the blessing of living abundantly, and from caring for our neighbor;

One: Yet you, Servant of all, came into our conversation precisely to show us the secret and source of joy-filled living

Many: By serving others, by trusting you to meet our needs, and by giving ourselves in care and sacrifice!

One: Call us back, dear Friend, to the thoughts and actions that bring us into your will and closer to the richness of life,

Many: That we may find our way, again, into the paths of righteousness and peace, rest beside still waters, and restoration for our souls!

Lead Scripture: Ezekiel 34:11-16 and John 10:11-16

Sermon Meditation: "Of Shepherds and Sheep"
So many people wander through life with no direction or purpose, as sheep without a shepherd; God has chosen to be a compassionate and safe shepherd to God's people; we are called to become compassionate, safe, and caring shepherds, just as God is

Pastoral Prayer

Listen this morning to our anxious thoughts, dear God, and quiet our stirring fears. We sometimes struggle to be honest with you because we fear your rejection. Remind us, please, that your grace overshadows your judgment and that forgiveness brought you to us, again, in Jesus Christ. We have little understanding of the kind of love that sacrifices, that places others before ourselves, that meets us in the darkness when we cannot find our way. Help us learn from you about the power of grace and reconciliation; teach us how to set aside our preconceptions and quick judgments in favor of a generous outlook toward brothers and sisters in our family; magnify our potential to do good, act responsibly, and provide mercy and hope in a world of apathy and distrust, we pray in your most Holy Name. Amen.

The Second Sunday of Lent

Meditation of Preparation

Before there's light
There may be dark,
So light can have its day;
Before there's life
There may be death,
So life can have its say;
Before there's hope
There may be dread,
Till lifeless dreams
May breathe, ahead!

Call to Affirmation and Commitment

Leader: We've come to find our focus and to draw strength from you, dear Maker.

People: Meet us, please, in the challenges and pressures of our lives.

Leader: Priorities quite soon lose their attraction, and vitality gives way to fatigue.

People: Take from our souls the stress ignited by anxious and unrealistic demands;

Leader: Remove the unneeded burden, the oppressive thought, the despairing point of view;

People: Increase the peaceful pause, the serene perspective, the joyful outlook;

Leader: Erase the doubt that undermines hope, the boredom that infects engagement, the worry that distracts us from the miracle in every day;

All: And call us once again into your enterprise of grace, to rise to higher standards, and to live in a closer walk with all you will and bless!

Lead Scripture: Micah 6:6-8 and Matthew 4:18-22

Sermon Meditation: "Follow the Leader"

The spiritual journey on earth has many treacherous turns; followers can soon become discouraged and disheartened in troubled places; God has promised to act as a companion in treacherous places, and asks us to also share the light and presence we have found with others

Pastoral Prayer

We've lost sight of your gentle and saving way, Shepherd Friend. Each week the frenzy of schedules and the requirements of living blur our vision, and discouragement and drudgery crowd out the confidence and contentment with which the day began. Refresh our capacity to see the way you lead us through, and quiet the noises that drown out your steady and compassionate voice. Forgive our lack of commitment and fidelity to your purposes, and retool our skills to forge behaviors that reflect your image and your love. Through Jesus Christ, companion in the darkness and the light always, we pray. Amen.

The Third Sunday of Lent

Meditation of Preparation

How many times will faith
Come knocking at my door?
How many illusions hide
The way to certainty?
How many changes are required
In each religious quest?
Is there another promised land—
Or is this where I am now?

Responsive Affirmation of Faith

Leader: In the rhythm of worship, generous Maker, this is the
    moment where we're struck by the kindness of your heart!

People: You provide the air we breathe, the water that quenches, the earth that nurtures,

Leader: The light for labor, and the night for rest; teach us to recognize your gifts to us each day!

People: Prompt us to trust you with tomorrow, and give us courage to embrace the unknown.

Leader: Grant us serenity of purpose, poise in crises, and a peace that surpasses understanding.

People: Continue to provide the cloud by day, the fire by night, the bread from heaven,

Leader: The path through troubled waters, and the fountain in the desert.

People: Accept our humble gratitude for all we have received, for all we've learned, and for the love and care we hold!

Lead Scripture: Genesis 12:1-4 and John 3:1-10

Sermon Meditation: "The Challenge of Faith"
Invitations to faith come to us several times in a lifetime; faith also develops and grows as many chapters in our personal story; mature faith is a set of beliefs tested over time, which grow in confidence and serenity

Pastoral Prayer

We stand uneasy in the midst of mystery, Spirit Divine. We seek certainty as a daily condition for any risks or invitations we may follow, and we bristle when our prayers are not answered immediately. As creatures already suspicious of what we cannot see or understand, we hesitate to follow unless we can be given guarantees of comfort and predictable results. Remind us, please, that every day is a gift—and a mystery itself! Reframe our minds and hearts to learn to trust you with the unknown, and to follow when the way is not clear, and to believe that you will remain with us through pain and sorrow, surprise and confusion, unsteadiness and doubts. Teach us to walk in faith with confidence and peace of mind; remove the barriers we impose on trusting you, and give us courage to try new opportunities and to stretch our capacity to believe. We pray in Jesus' name, for his sake and ours. Amen.

The Fourth Sunday of Lent

Meditation of Preparation

Does the darkness in the soul
Leave little room for dawn?
Does the sun delay to rise?
What does it take
To doubt my doubts?
Remove the shadows,
Prince of Light!

Call to Light and Life

Leader: The people who walked in darkness have seen a great light;

People: Yet, before the light, there is much darkness that surrounds us!

Leader: Dispel the shadows that assail us, Light of Nations.

People: Step into the chaos of our daily routine, and speak the word of clarity and order.

Leader: Part the waters that overpower us, and divide our day

People: Between labor and rest, sorrow and joy, struggle and peace.

Leader: Shed light upon every darkened path on which we've stumbled,

People: And illumine ways to find abundant living!

Leader: Forgive our faults, dispel our failures, and return the dawn

People: That sheds the light by which we follow safely and are able to recognize the everlasting grace of your embrace!

Lead Scripture: Exodus 24:15-18 and 2 Peter 1:19b-21

Sermon Meditation: "Until the Day Dawns in Your Heart"
We are creatures of darkness and light; we never shed the darkness completely, and we need help to overcome it; the Spirit of God provides light, courage, and power to help us overcome the darkness and follow Christ

Pastoral Prayer

We travel sometimes in the shadows, God of Light. We mean to follow in your path and live for what you value—yet we often fail, walk in circles, confused by many detours, consumed by suspicion, apprehension, and an awareness of our own inadequacy. We confess that we are too easily distracted and disillusioned by the challenges we face. We need your light, your encouragement, and your steadiness to overcome our fragile steps. Please forgive us for believing too little, for taking easier roads, and for aspiring for a fraction of who we might become. Transform our lethargy into a zest to do your bidding, to bring about your will on earth, and to bring light and hope into dark corners and despairing hearts, we pray, in Jesus' name. Amen.

The Fifth Sunday of Lent

Meditation of Preparation

An often angry world
Bids me unwelcome in its midst;
I've wandered, trying to belong,
Outside, wanting inside,
Feeling unwanted, often set aside . . .
Still waiting for an open door,
I stare at those who live within:
May I come in?

Call to Confession and Community

Leader: We are scattered and often disconnected members of one body, Maker of Families.

People: Assembled here to worship, work together, heal together, learn to love,

Leader: We come from isolated walks, busy schedules, sometimes lonely places,

People: To find a people with whom to belong, and a place for community, cooperation, common faith and ground.

Leader: We seek you because you have found us and called us to belong!

People: We seek each other because we have been loved, and called into a family.

Leader: Teach us again to erase the isolation we create for each other; help us break dividing walls;

People: Call us also to welcome the uninvited, to invite the forgotten, to embrace the unforgiven and neglected,

All: That we may walk in grace, practice hospitality, live as community, and follow your including ways!

Lead Scripture: Psalm 146:5-9 and Mark 10:13-16

Sermon Meditation: "Welcoming the Unwelcome?"
The family of God was designed to offer a safe and caring community for every pilgrim; the community of faith sometimes acts as a rejecting or closed network of people; Christ wants the body of Christ to reflect his welcome, friendship, and love to all

Pastoral Prayer

We were once not included, feeling uninvited, living on the outside, Bridge Maker God. We remember wondering if we belonged at all, and struggling to believe that we were welcome. Remind us here and now that you have built no walls, but came in Jesus Christ to build bridges of hope and forgiveness. Teach us to note that nothing can separate us from the love of God, and that we are commissioned to proclaim and deliver that message and reality to neglected and forgotten persons who doubt their value and importance—to you or to anyone! Prompt us to receive the good news of your grace and to transmit its hope and healing to people who still feel outside the barriers we so often build to keep your children out. Help us to welcome the child, the anxious, the wounded, the different soul, and the forgotten pilgrim on the road—to help them know that they belong to you and to us. For your sake and for our sake, we pray. Amen.

The Sixth Sunday of Lent

Meditation of Preparation

She bends, she draws the water
Which will quench her lips but not
Her soul; she walks away, refilled
But not restored. I, too,
Hold out an empty hand,
Connected to an empty soul—
And wish somehow to be refilled,
Some way to be restored,
Somehow to be made whole!
Where is the Well?

Call to Search and Discovery

Leader: Like a deer thirsting after cool water, we seek your face and presence, Lord of Bethlehem.

People: As the dry land longs for rain, so our parched souls seek the water of Life!

Leader: Restore the springs of hope that sustain our spirits, dear Messiah.

People: Make of us the well that holds the water, the soil upon which streams may flow,

Leader: The sheltering tree that provides the shade for weary travelers,

People: The home for those who've lost their home, the welcome voice, the steady hand.

Leader: Grant us once again a vision of your purpose, a sure knowledge of your presence,

People: And the reassuring awareness of your guidance and strength through the wilderness nearby!

Lead Scripture: Exodus 17:3-7 and John 4:7-15

Sermon Meditation: "If All Else Fails, Read the Directions"
Pilgrims in life are constantly in search of meaning, grace, and hope; we travel many miles with sometimes empty hearts and fewer hopes; Christ seeks us out to fill our hearts and life with purpose, joy, and peace

Pastoral Prayer

We possess much and have so little, Savior Friend. Our lives are full, and often feel so empty; we've come again, seeking the water that will quench our restlessness and restore the inner soul! Help us again to find the secret of abundant life while we're still living, Lord. We worry too much about things that may never happen, and cheat ourselves out of enjoying the present moment and your invitations to fullness and joy. Repair our worn and lifeless efforts by restoring purpose and value to our pointless ventures. Remind us that your well is nearby and that you offer us replenishment and refreshment at every turn, and grace and rest in places that need it most. In your most Holy Name, we pray. Amen.

The Seventh Sunday of Lent

Meditation of Preparation

I've heard it all, but also
Have not heard it well;
I've seen it all, and yet
Have failed to see;

I once imagined more, but now
Imagine less. Could there be more?

Call to Discovery and Discipleship

Leader: Thank you for waiting while we slowly awaken to your extravagant generosity, Creator God.

People: You, who spread the heavens and the earth, colored both, and gave us seasons,

Leader: Each for our enjoyment and awareness; how majestic is your touch!

People: You, who called forth mountains from seas, capped them with snows and trees,

Leader: Outlined the sunset, and invented sound; you, who gave the world more flavors

People: To the tongue than names can call; and placed more fish within an ocean

Leader: Than a mind can count! You, inventor of ideas, and wonders of the mind,

People: Which still is less than half explored!

Leader: You, designer of the higher gifts of care, faith, joy, commitment, grace, and value;

People: You, who dared to share them all with us, who have thus been blessed beyond all measure!

Lead Scripture: Genesis 15:1-5 and Luke 13:30-35

Sermon Meditation: "When Faith Is a Stumbling Block"
What we have believed can interfere with God's next revelation; God's revelation is an ongoing insight and call; Christ often invites us from a beginning belief to a deeper walk of faith

Pastoral Prayer

Dear Friend of the helpless and the dejected: We bring our preoccupations and distresses to your altar table, convinced that you care enough to listen, and to respond with compassion and healing. We are still astonished that you chose to live among us, walk beside us, love us, and forgive us when we do not love you back! You make our burdens lighter by your care and perspective; you sustain us with your kindness and grace; you uplift us with your faith in us, and model fidelity toward us when we break promises and fail to live up to your hopes for us. We confess that we are so concerned with our own safety and comfort that we forget what you have shown us—that the greatest reward comes in placing the needs of others at the center of our actions.

The Eighth Sunday of Lent

Meditation of Preparation

I compromised again today,
Drew back, stood still,
And turned away when I saw wrong . . .
Tomorrow I will come again
But dare myself to take a stand
Because my faith informs my step,
And courage calls me to affirm
What I believe, and know, is right!

Call to Fidelity and Commitment

Leader: We are a people prepared to remember the past, and sometimes tempted to relive it!

People: Free us, Savior Shepherd, from the tyranny of poor habits and haunting recollections;

Leader: Reassemble our priorities, divided and weakened by compromise and comfort;

People: Realign our dreams, dismantled and scattered in the struggle to survive each day;

Leader: Reorder our commitments, upended in the marketplace of shallow choices;

People: Reshape our perspective, stretched and worn from competing allegiances;

Leader: Remold our hearts to care and comfort as you do, and to do your will;

People: Remake our hands, to serve you and your family, and to bless as you bless!

Lead Scripture: Jeremiah 31:31-34 (or Malachi 3:16-18) and Luke 21:16-19

Sermon Meditation: "Taking Good Risks"
Each time we make decisions, we choose mostly between risks; the risk of not choosing is sometimes the greater risk; God asks us to risk "wisely" to accomplish God's will

Pastoral Prayer

Dear Covenant Maker: We've returned to restate vows we've voiced in these halls, too soon forgotten. We've promised much, done little, and even now we wonder if you will take us seriously when we ask to start over every time! We're here to confess that we usually know what is right but don't always choose it, that we often know your will but don't always want to follow it. We're also afraid to give of ourselves to worthy causes, or to a neighbor, or to you; we hold back, knowing that there is more in us to develop, to share, to grow, than we are often willing to allow. Please forgive our hesitation to trust you, our willingness to doubt you, our stubbornness to believe in you and follow. We invite you again to touch our troubled spirits and heal their striving; we ask you to transform our weak determination into reservoirs of eagerness and strength. We ask all this in the name of the one who came into our lives in an unassuming stable, and gave us so much more than we deserved—Jesus Christ, our Friend. Amen.

The Season of Easter

Palm Sunday

Meditation of Preparation

To grasp a deeper truth—
To hear beyond the words
And understand; to seek and find
A ray of light, an insight almost lost;
To seize a new dimension, available
But often missed! Is that
What he was trying to show me,
Before they nailed him to that tree?

Call to Confession and Understanding

Leader: Today we've joined the multitude that cheers you on, pale Conqueror.

People: Tomorrow we may join another crowd and cry for you to die.

Leader: We confess again that we still seek the easy road, the comfortable task, the painless labor.

People: We eagerly embrace any salvation that requires nothing from us, and shout hosannas,

Leader: And quickly scatter when our faith demands some sacrifice!

People: We want our enemies destroyed, freedoms restored, and little expected from us.

Leader: Help us find a better way to follow, a higher ground to cover, a more responsible vow.

People: Teach us to care, even at the cost of pain; to choose the road to peace, not war—

Leader: And grace us when we fall behind and stop, and fail to understand.

People: Sustain us with your gentle strength, guide us through the maze of alluring choices to the vision you want for us;

All: And help us don the mantle of forgiveness, peace, and reconciliation, that your kingdom and will may be done on earth as it is in heaven!

Lead Scripture: Zechariah 4:6 and Matthew 4:1-11

Sermon Meditation: "The Price of Following"
Christ's standards challenge many inadequate habits and traditions; followers can face misunderstanding, rejection, and anger; Christ faced the same unjust challenges and comforts and will sustain courageous believers who follow in his way and will

Pastoral Prayer

Did you really mean to walk into our lives and call us to a higher road of peace and grace? Do you understand our attraction to hostility and revenge as answers to injustice and pain? Can you help us with the caring anger we feel toward betrayal, abuse, and injury? Can you really show us a better way to deal with the unfairness and wounding found in this harsh world we live in? Please help us not to add to the problems and pain of your children. Our faces do not always betray the sadness and the dismay we feel inside; we need relief from uncaring attitudes and selfish postures. Rekindle hope within us, quenched by apathy and worry. Refresh our purposes with a sense of fulfillment and peace of mind, and add determination to our fading efforts to follow you. Spark a new eagerness to bring peace into troubled hearts, and guide us to love in your most perfect way, we pray. Amen.

Easter Sunday

Meditation of Preparation

I'm often found
Behind a busy frenzy
In the dark, afraid that when I stop,
I'll find myself.
Yet past the darkest moments
In my soul, a dawn
Is born, to let me know
That there is more ahead!
Press on, my soul, run to an empty grave,
Embrace the piercing light—
Warm to a living Son!

Responsive Call to Celebration

Leader: The shadows of a dying day have introduced the reign of death and defeat,

People: Yet the darkness fails to have a final word; a dim but steady light appears

Leader: Across the brooding sky. Creation waits again; it has known chaos and despair before;

People: It also felt the breath of God upon the dark, and heard the sound of One at work!

Leader: Behind the mystery, like the first morning, first a faint sky appeared;

People: Then the song of a bird, then the movement of God upon the chaos and upon a grave!

Leader: Creation, once again on tiptoe, leaned into the darkness, looking for the Source.

People: We creatures, often also waiting in the darkness, lean and listen, eager for the music,

Leader: Which declares that God is giving birth to life again, and in a newer frame:

People: Here, the rush of wind, the breath of God; there, breaking through the clouds, the rising sun;

Leader: Here, a stone, rolled aside by the power of Life, calling forth a Son;

People: There, in a quiet garden, death begins to die. The power of darkness shrinks, and the miracle of life walks from a grave!

Leader: He is alive! We are alive! Death is no more! Where, O death, is your victory?

People: Where, O death, is your sting? The sting of death is sin, but thanks to be to God,

Leader: Who gives us the victory through our Lord Jesus Christ! (Adapted from 1 Corinthians 15:55-56)

Lead Scripture: Job 19:23-27 and John 20:1-7a

Sermon Meditation: "Everyone's Dawn"
Life provides experiences that thrust us into both belief *and* disbelief; there are significant moments in our journey when we feel defeated and lost; in conquering death, Christ has shown us the presence and the way to hope again, a stunning sunrise and resurrection

Pastoral Prayer

Can you break through the clouds that surround us and beam a light of resurrection inside our darkened hopes? Can you call us from graveside dreams and dying aspirations to a dawn of fullness and new beginnings? Will you roll away the stone that blocks our view of what is most important, and of you, and of what we can believe? Will you still have patience with us when we fail to wait for you and struggle with our faith? Can you bring back to life the plans and commitments we have too soon abandoned, and equip us with anticipation and determination? Will you resurrect fidelity, care, and focus? We need to know that you are still at work in every graveside and in our hearts, dear Lord. For our sake, and for your will on earth, we pray. Amen.

The Second Sunday of Easter

Meditation of Preparation

The scattered group, like us
Assembled, once again—
Their purpose, in an upper room
We're told, was to continue
What he started; but they are
Still afraid, and locked
Away from causes he fought for . . .
And are we too
Afraid to follow?

Call to Reflection and Praise (inspired by Psalm 118:19ff)

Leader: Open to us, risen Savior, the gates of just living,

People: That we may enter, praise your name, and follow.

Leader: Is this not the gate of the Lord, where the righteous are invited to enter?

People: We give you thanks for delivering us and for making a way through the valley!

Leader: The stone that the builders rejected has become the chief cornerstone.

People: This is the Lord's doing; it is a marvelous thing and a strong hope.

Leader: This is the day that the Lord has made;

People: Let us exult and be glad in it! Even so, come forth again, dear One who saves, into our hearts!

Lead Scripture: Job 42:1-6 and John 20:19-23

Sermon Meditation: "Upper Room Jitters"
Anxieties and struggles challenge faith; contradictory emotions are welcome in worship; the invitation to believe again takes all our emotions seriously

Pastoral Prayer

We've come again into this space with many different thoughts and feelings, Risen One. We are at once astounded that you've conquered death and fearful that it may not be the case. Can you accept our struggle even now, in here? Can you help us quiet the unsteadiness that whispers doubt into our faulty steps and thoughts? Calm the waters that can drown good faith, and restore the peace that knows and believes that you can conquer every malady and injustice this world can conjure. Free us also from the apathy that concludes that our lives and our actions do not matter and cannot make a difference. Resurrect the dormant threads of abundant living, and lead us past the valley of indifference and death to your abundance of life. Through Christ, who conquered death, we pray. Amen.

The Third Sunday of Easter

Meditation of Preparation

Agreements made
May soon be lost,
And easy promises expressed
May rarely be delivered.
Why then renew a vow? Perhaps
In order to recall
A choice made long ago, and truth
Revalued and affirmed?

Call to Awareness and Worship (from Psalm 33)

Leader: The word of the Lord holds true, and God's works endure.

People: The Maker of life loves righteousness and justice;

Leader: God's love unfailing fills the earth!

People: We have waited eagerly for the God of hope.

Leader: God is our help and shield;

People: In God our hearts are glad; our trust is in a holy name!

Leader: May thy unfailing love, dear Maker, rest upon us, surround us, and sustain us,

People: For we have placed our faith and hope in you!

Lead Scripture: Jeremiah 32:36-41 and Revelation 5:7-10

Sermon Meditation: "Renewing Vows"

Biblical covenants and vows are designed to help us take certain issues and commitments seriously; choosing and voicing promises and vows define a believer's faith; faithfulness to vows and covenants reflects the character, dependability, and authority of those who promise

Pastoral Prayer

You were the first to utter promises, O Master of covenants. You stepped into your creation, made us all, and promised us abundant living, a flowering of purposes, and joy. We've returned to hear those promises again and to remake some vows ourselves. Remind us here and now that you have promised that you will not abandon us or leave us to our own designs without help. Strengthen our capacity to believe and to make commitments ourselves—to you and to one another! Quicken our capacity to remain faithful to important vows we've made. Focus our understanding on the value of careful covenants and on the gift you offer us in modeling sacred commitments. Forgive us for floundering in our resolve to follow your ways, and grant us second chances in our failed attempts to do your will, we pray. Amen.

The Fourth Sunday of Easter

Meditation of Preparation

Invited to a feast
I am forever clutching
Morsels; promised an abundance
I'm left wanting
When the door is closed.
How do I discover
The unending source of satisfaction
Sketched by the Creator
At the start? Are there clues
To finding the abundant life?

Responsive Call to Discovery (adapted from Psalm 55)

Leader: Come, all you who are thirsty, come to the waters!

People: Come, you who have no food, come and buy, not for money, and without a price!

Leader: Why do we spend our money on that which is not bread,

People: And our labor for that which does not satisfy?

Leader: Listen, and we will have good food to eat, and we will enjoy the richness of the land.

People: Come to me, and listen to my words; hear me, and you shall have life, says Yahweh,

Leader: I will make a covenant with you, this time for life.

People: Inquire of the Lord God while he may be found, call upon him while he is near.

All: Even so, Sustainer, Redeemer, come into our lives!

Lead Scripture: Job 28:12-18 and Matthew 13:44-46

Sermon Meditation: "Are We Getting What We Paid For?"
We all strive for personal meaning and fulfillment in life; we often struggle with a stubborn emptiness and meaninglessness, looking for

fulfillment in inadequate sources; we can only find ultimate fulfillment in God's purpose of abundant life

Pastoral Prayer

Here at your altar we seek again the source of deepest joy and meaning, Creator Friend. We have been busy searching for the secret of abundant life. What can fill our hearts and minds with lasting satisfaction? Our hands have labored long and still are empty. We've stumbled over our possessions, found them inadequate, and turn to you again to solve the mystery: How do we fill the vacant places in our souls? What have we lost, or never had? Replenish purpose and direction, please, that we may find the way to the peace and joy you intended in your garden. Quiet our fears that you no longer care for us, and lead us again to pleasant pastures and beside still waters, for your sake and ours, we pray. Amen.

The Fifth Sunday of Easter

Meditation of Preparation

Faith is first, most likely,
Just a word; adorned,
In time, it grows to feeble strength;
Challenged by small adversities
It buds, and shows the promise
Of becoming an adequate companion
In the valleys where the shadows
Make their deepest scars!

Responsive Call to Faith

Leader: We have walked sometimes in darkness, and have seen a great light;

People: Those who live in the valley of the shadow of death have seen the Face of light.

Leader: Send out your light, Creator God; send forth your truth,

People: For your word is a lamp to our feet, a light to our path!

Leader: A light shines in the darkness, and the darkness has not overcome it;

People: For the Lord God is our light, and our salvation!

Lead Scripture: Psalm 23:1-4 and Mark 9:20-24

Sermon Meditation: "Faith in the Valleys"
Genuine faith still harbors bouts with doubt; evaluating imperfect and undeveloped faith can be a step toward stronger belief; Christ meets us and assists in growing a faith that survives spiritual valleys

Pastoral Prayer

Dear God, we struggle between certainty and fear, faith and doubt, hope and disillusionment; in the absence of clarity, we lose confidence; in the silence during which there are no answers, suspicion and fear often increase. Please continue to accept us as fragile believers who waver daily in our fidelity and determination to believe and follow you. Please work gracefully in our confusion, and walk with us through the uncertainties and injustices in life. Call us gently to believe above the questions that haunt and tease us in troubling times. Bring peace to bear upon our anxieties, and remind us that faith sometimes is born where clarity and certainty cannot be found. Through Christ we pray. Amen.

The Sixth Sunday of Easter

Meditation of Preparation

In this quiet, holy space,
Lonely people often gather,
Seeking solace, an embrace,
And answers to their deepest
Questions. Pilgrims come
In different shapes;
So do friends, and faith that matters.

Can You see inquiring faces—
Heal the wounds, and still the clatter?

Call to Worship and Search

Leader: The Lord reigns; the Lord God rules forever!

People: We are clothed in weakness; our days are brief.

Leader: God is robed in strength; the Almighty is from generation to generation.

People: Though the floods surround us, we will trust.

Leader: Though the hills and the trees be moved,

People: Yet will we trust; our strength and our redemption are from God.

Leader: Teach us to trust your ways; help us to find your path, Sustainer God,

People: That we may know your love, your peace, your purpose in our lives!

Lead Scripture: Ecclesiastes 4:8-12 and Ephesians 2:17-22

Sermon Meditation: "Aliens and Community"
All of us were designed by God for relationship and community; isolation and suspicion can trump community; the family of God was designed to create relationship, trust, and community

Pastoral Prayer

We quietly long for safe relationships and love, dear God; yet we so often feel excluded, or exclude ourselves, from love and belonging! Help us find fellowship and comfort in the right places, Master of relationships, and assist us to give double effort to the cause of caring for others. Shape us here into a family of brothers and sisters committed to your will; clothe us in compassion and kindness, and make us a shelter for the traveler facing storms and isolation—that we may be the body of Christ still active in this often cruel world. We pray in your name, and for our sake, Amen.

The Seventh Sunday of Easter

Meditation of Preparation

What I inherit I received
From someone else;
What I pass on depends
On what I myself embrace:
I shape today, and soon reframe tomorrow;
Am I a miser with today—
Or will I grace tomorrow?

Call to Worship and Reflection (adapted from Psalm 20)

Leader: May the Lord God answer when we call, or are distressed;

People: May the name and character of Jacob's God protect us!

Leader: May God send us help and guidance in the sanctuary, and grant us support;

People: May God remember best intentions, and our prayers of faith;

Leader: May the Lord God grant us the desires of our heart, and make our plans succeed,

People: As long as they are grounded in and informed by God's will and way.

Leader: We will then be blessed and shout for joy, for the God of love!

People: May the Lord God grant us wisdom and hear our requests!

Lead Scripture: Ruth 2:4-9 and Galatians 6:7-10

Sermon Meditation: "Paying It Forward?"
We daily have received grace, hope, love, and peace; what we have received becomes a blessing and gift to be passed on; by God's will and generosity we become carriers of good news to a waiting world.

Pastoral Prayer

We confess that our prayers and requests of you are often immature and shallow, Redeemer Friend. We sometimes ask for what will please immediately, with little grasp of any longer effects. We seek relief before we learn from challenge; we petition, but we fail to ask for what you deem is best. Teach us again the dialogue of prayer. Help us learn the value of seeking your wisdom and perspective; reduce our anxieties about the moment, and give us better vision for the pleas we utter without due reflection. Thanks for listening carefully to us and for ignoring vain requests that harm us. Prompt us to consider the greater good and the concerns of others, that our prayers may not be selfish ambition or self-serving speeches. Purge our anxieties and double our faith, we pray, in your most holy name. Amen.

The Season of Pentecost

Pentecost Sunday

Meditation of Preparation

Is God away? The awesome
Presence appears absent
From the daily course of life . . . .
Is it because
I've lost the sense of fear and awe
When God is near?
Can I, who revere little,
Ever pause and wonder
At the mystery I cannot comprehend?

Call to Wonder and Reflection (adapted from Genesis 1 and John 1)

Leader: In the beginning God created the heavens and the earth.

People: In the beginning was the Word, and the Word was with God, and the Word was God.

Leader: And the earth was without form and void, and darkness was upon the face of the deep.

People: In God was life, and the life was the light of all; and the light shines in the darkness.

Leader: And the darkness did not understand it.

People: Give us eyes to see, and ears to hear, O One who brings us light!

Lead Scripture: Genesis 3:20-24 and Matthew 11:25-30

Sermon Meditation: "Are You There?"
The Presence of God each day is a biblical affirmation; the Spirit is a mystery to our senses and is sometimes difficult to comprehend; God's Spirit works mysteriously in us and in our world—in ways too wonderful to fully understand

Pastoral Prayer

We avoid mysteries and worship clarity and certainty, Spirit God. How can we fathom a Presence we cannot palpably understand? How can we apprehend that which is far beyond our meager senses? We strive to believe in your Spirit's presence in a distressing and disturbing world, dear God; we see injustice and callousness at every turn, and we hope that you will intervene and reverse the evil that appears to preside and control what is good! Is there a tangible way to tap into your power and presence—for ourselves and for others? Will you enter the hollow places in our own lives, where apathy and cynicism prevail and selfishness has its day—and transform us? Can you stifle the propensity to do harm and the attraction to violence as a way of solving differences? In what ways can we contribute to peace and to hope? Give us a measure of your wisdom, Maker of good gifts, so that we may become instruments of healing and peace. In the name of your greatest gift, Jesus Christ, we pray. Amen.

The First Sunday after Pentecost

Meditation of Preparation

Life provides
Shadow and surprise,
Clarity and confusion,
Comfort and distress;
Stern occasions

Strain the soul, and test the seam of sanity.
Such times also force
Our weakness to the surface, unadorned.
And then? Then we face
Our frazzled faith—and
Someone else's strength!

Call to Confession and Celebration

Leader: We've come to you again with frayed and tattered hopes, O Lord of wonder.

People: Our dreams have shrunk, our plans have dimmed, our faith has wavered.

Leader: We are driven and pressed by duty and expectation.

People: We are burdened and distressed by goals we cannot reach.

Leader: We feel unable, inadequate, ill-equipped to rise above our failures.

People: Yet you have met us here before, to fortify and strengthen!

Leader: Remain the steady hand in our uncertain moments;

People: Become the faithful Spirit in unfaithful times;

Leader: Hold together worthy dreams and hopes we fail to hold!

People: Encourage us that we may once again take heart, walking in confidence and courage because you walk beside us,

Leader: And celebrate that we walk the road of hope and deepest joy!

Lead Scripture: Psalm 102:1-7 and Mark 14:32-42

Sermon Meditation: "Stress and Strength"
The daily walk brings challenge and stress; we often become distressed and discouraged by such burdens—and face our limitations; the power of Christ and the Spirit of God enable us to conquer inadequacy and distress

Pastoral Prayer

You know our hearts enough to know that sometimes we come limping in to see your face and hear your voice, dear Friend. Fatigue and fear affect the nerve and pulse of every try, and we too soon are overwhelmed and worn. We need to know that you are present when we falter; we need to hear that you care for us when we've lost the way. We seek your mercy and your patience for our trying times, and bread and water for our parched and used-up hopes. Clear our minds of defeating thoughts and excessive expectations, we pray; reduce the weight of our self-imposed requirements, and bring your mercy to bear gently on our worries. Lift us up by your grace to see a hopeful vision of life lived in your care, and sustain us when we need to rest and fill our cups—with peace. Through Christ, our friend, we pray. Amen.

The Second Sunday after Pentecost

Meditation of Preparation

Great occasions are both made
And lost: Every day
A sterling invitation goes unnoticed,
Casually replaced
By trivial pursuit; have I lately
Missed a rich experience
While distracted by light fare?

Call to Awareness and Exploration (adapted from Isaiah 62:10ff)

Leader: Go through, go through the gates, prepare the way for the people;

People: Build up, build up the highway, clear it of stones;

Leader: Raise up a sign for the people;

People: This is the Lord God's proclamation, to the ends of the earth:

Leader: Tell the daughter of Zion, behold, your salvation comes!

People: God carries a reward for all the people,

Leader: And they shall be called a holy people, the redeemed of Yahweh.

People: You shall also be called the "long sought," a city and people not forsaken.

Leader: Even so, Almighty God, show us the way to redemption and light!

Lead Scripture: Exodus 32:1-4 and Matthew 22:1-6

Sermon Meditation: "Trivial Pursuit?"
We spend much time in trivial and shallow pursuits; assessing what we spend our time on and how we spend it is important; followers of the Spirit are commissioned to spend time on what really matters to God

Pastoral Prayer

We become distracted by many preoccupations and superficial detours, dear God; too quickly we lose sight of priorities and roads of choice, and we follow side paths that waste our energy and time. Please call us back to the main events that offer purpose and service in your way and name. Remind us of our original, carefully chosen commitments and pursuits, and free us from the tyranny of shallow issues and unworthy exercises. Call us also to the higher ground that brings joy and hope into our lives, and that of others. Equip us to choose carefully how we spend the day, and grant us a measure of your wisdom in decisions that require patience and care. We pray through Christ, seeking your Spirit and way. Amen.

The Third Sunday after Pentecost

Meditation of Preparation

A hand, stretched out to give,
Returns unto itself—
But never empty!

A heart, prepared to love,
Is target, also, to the deepest
Satisfaction! And can we opt,
Or dare, for less?

Responsive Call to Worship (based on Isaiah 61 and Luke 4)

Leader: The Spirit of the Lord is upon us

People: Because he has anointed us to preach good news to the poor.

Leader: He has sent us to proclaim release to the captives

People: And recovery of sight to the blind;

Leader: To set at liberty those who are oppressed;

All: To proclaim the acceptable year of the Lord, the year for which everyone has been waiting!

Lead Scripture: Ezekiel 34:11-16 and Luke 10:30-37

Sermon Meditation: "When All Else Fails, Read the Directions"
God is like a healing shepherd tending wounded sheep; Christ came to set free the captive and the oppressed; we are called also to care for those who are mistreated and ignored

Pastoral Prayer

You found us, Shepherd God, when we were wandering and anxious. You have embraced us when we were afraid, sustained us when worn, upheld us when perplexed; you have also encouraged us when we were discouraged and affirmed us when we failed to believe in ourselves. You have imbued us with vigor and confidence, and placed us again on a safe path and a sure purpose. And now you equip us to find our brother and our sister, and release their burden, and bless their path with hope and care. Give us wisdom for the mission of touching others with your grace and healing power, and grant us a measure of joy for doing part of your will on earth, we pray, until we reach a day of total joy and peace at last. Amen.

The Fourth Sunday after Pentecost

Meditation of Preparation

I know the one who baffles me
The most—resides within!
What secrets lurk inside of me;
What forces are at work?
Am I the owner of my thoughts?
The only resident within?
And, if I have a mind and soul—
Am I entirely on my own?

Call to Confession and Grace

Leader: Again, we search for meaning and direction in this place, O holy God.

People: As you have searched for us, so we have sought your face!

Leader: We are but creatures of time and space, so we seek to see, to hear, to hold, and to touch.

People: Remind us once again that truth is real, yet beyond touch; that faith is strong, yet beyond proof.

Leader: Give us insight and imagination to see and understand you in new ways.

People: Give us wisdom to hear and touch the Mystery of your Presence.

Leader: Assure us that what we seek is not in vain; give us faith to find you in the invisible.

People: Touch our hearts in the puzzle of life, that we may receive you as a Holy Other!

Leader: Grant that we may walk in darkness, yet grasp a flicker of your light.

People: Teach us to wait in mystery, face the unknown expectantly, embrace uncertainty,

All: And find the Truth, the Way, and the Life!

Lead Scripture: Joel 2:28-29 and Luke 11:9-13

Sermon Meditation: "The Moving Presence"

The Spirit of God is a mysterious and unknown presence; we struggle to apprehend and believe in the Spirit's action and power within us; by faith we become instruments of grace and care as the Presence of God works in us and in our world

Pastoral Prayer

We fear what we cannot control or understand, dear Maker God. There are no ways to prove that you are present in our damaged world, let alone healing and inspiring beyond our comprehension, existing in the mystery of life itself. We are both afraid of and attracted by your power and apparent commitment to our welfare. Teach us to find peace in what we cannot fully understand and to trust in what we cannot explain or prove. We want to believe; help our disbelief. Erase our faith in suspicion and doubt, and restore a wider vision of your care among us. Forgive us for desiring certainty before we follow, and enlarge our capacity to work, love, and heal as you do in this disabled world. We pray in the name and nature of the One who came that we might know the God of love—Jesus Christ, our sustainer and friend. Amen.

The Fifth Sunday after Pentecost

Meditation of Preparation

Discarded gifts, abandoned
By neglect, they sit and wait
For keener eyes to know their worth;
Fussed over, argued about, but
Soon ignored, expensive treasures
Laid to waste by casual hands;
Misused and rusting? Useful still:
Freedom and choice!

Call to Confession and Hope

Leader: We have been enriched by the stunning gifts of freedom and choice, Maker of Life.

People: We are often casual with our freedom, we confess, and inactive with our choices.

Leader: Forgive us our sometimes shallow interest in liberty, for ourselves or others,

People: And our lip service to rights we rarely exercise.

Leader: Help us to distinguish between responsibility and futility, uselessness and usefulness,

People: That we may with integrity make use of freedom to work your worthy cause.

Leader: Teach us the higher use of choices that strengthen and improve us and our neighbors;

People: Save us from shallow, irresponsible freedom in our use of time and energy;

Leader: Call each of us to celebrate your awesome gift of freedom by acting in character with Christ;

People: Give us wisdom and insight into the proper stewardship of our unparalleled liberty and power—for good!

Lead Scripture: 1 Kings 19:8-11a and Galatians 5:1 (for the Sunday before July 4, or the next one below)

Sermon Meditation: "Beyond Slavery"
We have been blessed with an amazing freedom and a country where we are allowed many choices; freedom and choice provide opportunities both for responsible living and unfocused, wasteful living; the Christian's goal is to use freedom and choice as opportunities to serve God and God's people in ways that bring fulfillment and joy

Pastoral Prayer

We give you thanks, Creator God, for the amazing gifts of liberty, choice, and opportunity we share in this free nation. We are recipients of the privilege of freedom of worship, and we are allowed to use our time as we see fit. Assist us, we pray, to remember that our freedom is a means to do your will in the most unfettered ways. Remind us also that Christ deserves our highest loyalty and commitment. Help us remember that our greatest gift as patriots to our nation is not to make idolatry of our allegiance to her but to offer our best mind and heart to her devotion, to pray to God for our country, and to commit to making it the place that honors Christ's call to follow him—expressed to every human being. Give us your discernment and guidance each day, Maker God, on how to serve God and country responsibly, that we may employ our time and energy in ways that honor you! We pray through Christ, Amen.

The Sixth Sunday after Pentecost (closest to July 4th)

Meditation of Preparation

Few allegiances demand
The highest loyalties of life:
Family, fidelity to faith, and
Devotion to our country
Claim the highest call;
And how will a disciple—
Then or now—prioritize
Such loyalties and
Keep faith with each vow?

Call to Worship and Responsibility (adapted from Psalm 127 and 128)

Leader: Unless the Lord God builds the house,

People: Those who build it labor in vain.

Leader: Unless the Lord God watches over the city,

People: The watchman stays awake in vain.

Leader: It is in vain that you rise up early and go late to rest,

People: Eating the bread of anxious toil.

Leader: Blessed is everyone who fears Yahweh,

People: Who walks in his ways; you shall prosper, and it shall be well with you.

Lead Scripture: Esther 4:12-16 and Mark 12:13-17

Sermon Meditation: "Loyal to Caesar and to God?"
We each are called to take vows of allegiance to important causes and people; sometimes allegiance to God and allegiance to country may be at odds; the Christian's highest allegiance is to God

Pastoral Prayer

You have called us to be faithful and loyal to primary causes, and to you, dear God; give us courage and determination to make worthy commitments and to keep faithful to those obligations. Give us wisdom in the selection of people and causes to whom loyalties are due; give us insight and discernment when different loyalties force us to choose between them; and remind us that our greatest allegiance is to you above all others. Teach us, also, faithful God, how to become faithful and dependable in our vows. Give us both courage and integrity to make lasting and superior commitments in life. Give us also grace to understand the value and power of primary duties and the importance of fidelity in relationships. Remind us, if we forget, that we are to love our country but worship only you. Through Christ we pray. Amen.

The Seventh Sunday after Pentecost

Meditation of Preparation

Some things are well begun,
But left half done;
Some plans are half complete,
As goals abandoned
On the road half traveled.
And is the effort
In my life—half baked?

Call to Discernment and Focus

Leader: Truly, my life waits silently for God.

People: My hope of deliverance comes from Yahweh.

Leader: In truth, God is my rock of deliverance,

People: My tower of strength, so that I am unshaken!

Leader: Trust always in God, my people; pour out your heart before him.

People: God is our shelter; power belongs to God; and true love, O God, is from you!

Lead Scripture: Hosea 7:8-9 and Revelation 3:1-2

Sermon Meditation: "Half Baked?"
We begin some goals and projects with good intentions but are casual in our commitment to them; we can soon lose interest or focus, become less committed to causes that take time and effort; we are called to choose important causes and remain committed to their full completion under God

Pastoral Prayer

We have come to confess that we often seek the easy way and the comfortable enterprise, Holy God. You have called us to significant service and selective tasks, and we quickly grow tired of commitments that require our best effort and our greater care. Teach us again the value of hard work in the cause of worthwhile purposes; refocus our priorities to choose longer efforts that deliver richer rewards. Tune our hearts to follow where Christ has labored, to work in an enduring way for good, to bless the unblessed, to embrace the forgotten, to love the unloved, and to heal the wounded, that we might be your Presence in an often careless and even hostile world, and that we might complete goals we made promises to fulfill. We ask and pray in the name of the One who came to show us the way, Jesus Christ. Amen.

The Eighth Sunday after Pentecost

Meditation of Preparation

I'm not delivered
From my past!
Chained to my worst memories
And my regrets, I also
Drag an undelivered life:
Collected guilt,
Accumulated shame, and
Half-redeemed experiences
Lurk still beneath the surface . . . .
How can I be delivered?

Call to Worship and Affirmation (based on Psalm 40)

Leader: I waited patiently for the Lord;

People: He turned to me and heard my cry;

Leader: He drew me up from the desolate pit, out of the miry bog,

People: And set my feet upon a rock, making my steps secure.

Leader: He put a new song in my mouth, a song of praise.

People: I have told the glad news of deliverance to the great congregation;

Leader: I have not hid thy saving help within my heart.

People: I have spoken of thy faithfulness and thy salvation; I have not concealed thy steadfast love!

Lead Scripture: Isaiah 43:1-2; Romans 6:4; and Colossians 1:11-14

Sermon Meditation: "Deliverance"

We all carry guilt, regret, and shame over experiences in life; such burdens can become permanent weights that impede a journey of hope and love; Christ has promised that we are forgiven for our faults and sins, and called to walk in newness of life

Pastoral Prayer

We've come into this room seeking some grace, dear Friend. The burdens in our lives seem heavy, and at times we can't rid ourselves of oppressive memories and troubling thoughts. Can you forgive us for what we've failed to do? Will you forgive us for what we have done that we wish we had not? Does grace have a deadline? Are our faults held against us, since our memories will not leave them alone? How can we find the release and freedom you have promised us, so that we may not revisit our transgressions over and over? Grant us a lasting sense of your mercy, dear God, and a keen awareness of your grace, that our memories may be cleansed by the power of your forgiveness and love. Because of Christ, we plead and pray. Amen.

The Ninth Sunday after Pentecost

Meditation of Preparation

The road I travel
Carries many signs:
Some give direction, others
Warn of danger;
Some tell me where I am,
How far I have to go,
Or where the crossroads lie.
There, I make decisions,
Pick my destination,

Mark my progress, travel on . . .
What signs will I soon follow
On the crossroads of my life?

Call to Confession and Direction

Leader: We are like sheep without a shepherd, Lord of the valley.

People: You have not left us; we have been distracted, and have strayed . . . .

Leader: We have strayed from giving our best effort, from choosing the best,

People: From working in your causes of mercy, peace, and justice;

Leader: We have tried our own solutions, and failed; our own paths, and stumbled.

People: Show us again the path to forgiveness, to justice, to mercy, to peace!

Leader: Lead us again beside the still waters, and quiet our fears and restlessness.

People: Direct us to tread the greening pastures of your way, to follow the path that leads to your will.

Leader: Bind up our wounds, strengthen our frail limbs, straighten our burdened backs, uplift our weary hands and hearts,

People: That we may walk with the Good Shepherd and not grow weary; run, and tread the kingdom road!

Lead Scripture: Joshua 4:19-23a and Luke 15:3-32

Sermon Meditation: "Lost and Found"

The spiritual journey carries us through roads with many "signs"; we have choices as to which "markers" we follow; the road signs chosen make a vital difference in the spiritual journey we experience

Pastoral Prayer

There are so many signs to follow on the complicated journey of a lifetime, dear God. Overwhelmed by the number of conflicting messages along the way, we have ignored some warnings and been attracted to others of limited value. We confess how easily we are distracted by promises of easy living and quick detours to important concerns. We too frequently seek the cheaper discipleship and the safer road to travel. We focus mostly on ourselves and what will please us. Call us back to a way of living that includes commitment and purpose; give us discernment to choose carefully and wisely as we trudge the road; guide us around roadblocks and obstacles that obstruct our view of your will and your way; help us to trust that your call and direction is the only way to a fulfilling journey. We pray with hope and gratitude, Amen.

The Tenth Sunday after Pentecost

Meditation of Preparation

The taste is weak,
Its savor gone—
The strength suppressed
Adds little zest—
Its life is dull . . . What happened
To the force that turned
The world of values upside down?
Who tamed the tide?
Who doused the flame?
Can the lost flavor—be restored?

Call to Focus and Recovery

Leader: We know we have been called to be light!

People: We confess that our light is often dimmed, that we have not dispelled the darkness,

Leader: That we have also lost the way while were challenged to be salt.

People: We admit that we have lost our zest and have failed to add moral flavor to the world;

Leader: We have hidden our light and dulled our voice.

People: We are now back to restore our brightness, our taste, our usefulness;

Leader: Make us again a people of a higher flavor in the world!

People: Help us to carry your light, to be your moral fiber in this time and place,

Leader: That we may change the eyes and hearts of your people, so that we may all become your kingdom people here on earth!

Lead Scripture: Leviticus 2:13; Numbers 18:19; Mark 9:50; and Colossians 4:6

Sermon Meditation: "Salty People"

We've been summoned to make a difference in this world in the name of Christ; we often have acted and looked more like the world we want to change than like a model of change; Christ calls us to become the model of change, healing, joy, and redemption that he was

Pastoral Prayer

Dear Redeemer, you have invited us to make a qualitative difference in this world you created as a garden of hope and joy, and we have frequently resorted to delivering the same worn, ineffective messages that have failed your people before. Forgive us for not caring enough to announce the good news where there already is so much apathy and bad news. Remind us that we hold in our hands and hearts the same hope and grace your Son brought us as Jesus Christ, and that his gift and mercy create life and purpose in the most dreaded haunts of helplessness and hopelessness! Rekindle our desire to model compassion, forgiveness, and love in cynical places, and equip us to speak and live in such a way that people everywhere come to know the measure and power of your love and plan for each of us. Through Jesus Christ, our salt and Savior, we pray. Amen.

The Eleventh Sunday after Pentecost

Meditation of Preparation

With faltering steps
And fragile words,
She speaks the truth
In stammering tones—
Retreats, and cowers to the crowd;
Afraid to pioneer the new,
She still responds to God's strong hope,
That she will cradle, keep, and grow
The Savior's family on the road . . . .
Her name? The church!

Responsive Call to Community

Leader: We are a scattered people!

People: Called to live as family and work together,

Leader: We often isolate ourselves and work at odds with one another.

People: Call us again to become the people of your covenant, Creator God;

Leader: Reclaim us, that we may claim your vision and become your family.

People: Forgive us our propensity to live as if others do not matter.

Leader: Remind us that we have been carefully chosen, firmly commissioned, gracefully set aside

People: To be your people, who declare your praises by our way of life!

Leader: Still any restless hearts, quiet fears, renew hopes and focus,

People: And lead us on, that we may call out others from the darkness into your caring light!

Lead Scripture: Isaiah 57:14-15 and 1 Peter 2:2-10

Sermon Meditation: "Some Assembly Required"
God's people were created as a family to be a community of hope and love; the family of God has sometimes faltered, sometimes led in faith, sometimes avoided leading and sharing God's message and mission; we need to recover and renew our commission to be the body of Christ, doing his work and redeeming all into Christ's family

Pastoral Prayer

We know that we have been created and empowered to act as a family of hope and love in an uncaring and harsh world, Almighty God. Prompt us to embrace your children seeking a safe family. Grant us discernment to care for the abused, the lonely, the afraid, the ignored, and the helpless. Inspire us to aspire to become Christ's body, pausing to notice the unnoticed, kneeling to heal the harmed, and telling the truth when injustice presides. Cause us to become vulnerable in the name of love and care, as Christ was, and continue to transform us into a community of faith, sacrificial love, and unselfish regard. We pray as fearful followers who seek your will and way. Amen.

Twelfth Sunday after Pentecost

Meditation of Preparation

The recurring drama once again
Unfolds: The gathered people
Wait! And, I, beside them,
Also wait, and hope;
What do we hope for? Will we
Somehow be affected?
The music plays, a song is sung,
And oft repeated words are heard again . . . .
And why? Is there some magic

In the repetition? Is this
Another social hour—
Or what will occur?

Call to Worship and Revelation

Leader: We bring our wandering minds and hearts to you, O Living God.

People: Our thoughts rehearse our worries, and we make light of holy moments.

Leader: Teach us to harness the power and the potential of thoughts turned to worship and reflection.

People: Guide us to entertain imaginative and redemptive reflections of your Presence.

Leader: Our hearts have also wandered, fickle and easily distracted, frail and anxious;

People: Help us to channel motive and desire, interest and eagerness, to listen for your voice;

Leader: Help us keep our minds from idle and useless excursions.

People: Teach us the discipline of hearing your still, small voice and of learning to recognize you in creative silence.

Leader: Stir us in the moment to acknowledge that the ground on which we stand is holy,

People: That mind and heart and soul may here be quickened, and that we may worship You in truth, we pray!

Lead Scripture: Psalm 138:1-5 and Luke 4:16-21

Sermon Meditation: "What We Bring to Worship"

The hour of worship is designed for an encounter and dialogue between Creator and creature; the distractions, preoccupations, and attitudes we bring into the hour can inhibit our capacity to experience God's presence and the holy; training our minds and hearts to prepare to listen and focus in anticipation of holy moments will help us encounter and respond to the Divine

THE SEASON OF PENTECOST

Pastoral Prayer

Are we talking to ourselves, or is Someone listening? Are you already present and listening to us, Maker of Life? We come into this space saddled with concerns and worries; our capacity to focus is limited, we confess. And yet we want to discover a Presence and a Power that can overcome the smallness and the unimportant in our lives—and preside in us in a such a way that we are reassured that we are not alone and that there is hope beyond our feeble strength, to lead a better, purer life. We seek a greater confidence in you, O God, and a deeper faith and purpose for ourselves. We want to be empowered, directed, and enabled to live a worthy life! Help us to hear you over the noise we bring into this room. In the name of the One who came that we might have abundant life, Jesus Christ, we pray. Amen.

Thirteenth Sunday after Pentecost

Meditation of Preparation

A neighbor's hard to find
When I'm avoiding him;
My neighbor is the stranger who
Suddenly disturbs me
With his need—the uninvited
Traveler whose condition
Threatens how I planned to spend
My money or my time.
After all: Am I my neighbor's keeper?

Call to Responsibility and Care

Leader: We have been summoned to remember, Lord:

People: To recall that we all are children of a loving God, and siblings to one another.

Leader: Remind us that our work is to redeem and reconcile broken relationships, not to add division and distance between people.

People: Renew in us your Spirit of care and concern for members of your family whom we have failed to recognize as neighbors to our lives.

Leader: Teach us the value of every human being, and help us see the face of Christ in every face we meet.

People: Forgive us the self-preoccupation that blinds us to the need next door.

Leader: Disturb our apathy to human hurt, and rekindle in us a passion for the welfare of each of your children.

People: Give us Christ's eyes, and his heart, that we may also see and heal!

Lead Scripture: Leviticus 19:16-18 and Luke 10:29-37

Sermon Meditation: "Are You Looking for Trouble?"
God's view of family identifies our neighbor as our sibling; neighbors to us are the ones next to us who have a need that we can fill; Christ has called us to care for one another in keeping with Christ's love for us

Pastoral Prayer

We struggle with our own needs, God of Care, and sometimes wonder if they will overwhelm us. We become anxious about tomorrow and find it hard to think about anyone else when we are assaulted by the daily stress. Yet you have reminded us that you care for us, that you will take care of our needs, and that we need to trust you as a God of compassion and provision. Help us, then, to believe in your constancy and to focus on a neighbor as a person whose concerns are often far greater than our own.

Fourteenth Sunday after Pentecost

Meditation of Preparation

A very sad affliction
Has permanently disabled

My capacity to learn;
Also affected, at the time
Was my ability to grow . . . .
I myself imposed the damage
When I chose to close my mind.
Now I wonder: Can the damage
Be repaired? Can I still grow?

Call to Awareness and Reflection

Leader: We are here to confess and hope, Maker God:

People: We confess that we have failed your vision for us, closed our hearts to your intentions,

Leader: Turned away from your directions, ceased to learn, and traded openness for safety.

People: We have often closed our minds and our imaginations, blunted faith and growth;

Leader: Yet you continue to provide recovery and reversal to our folly!

People: You care enough for us not to leave us to small minds and hearts,

Leader: So open our eyes, that we may see life as you do;

People: Open our hearts, that we may love good and do good as you do;

Leader: Open our minds, that we may become wiser to your will;

People: Open our lives, that we may still be shaped and formed by your perfect purpose,

Leader: That we may join your song, find hope, and magnify your name!

People: Even so, come, Lord, release us captives and dwell among us!

Lead Scripture: Genesis 16:1-6 and Luke 13:31-34

Sermon Meditation: "Closed and Open Minds"
Human beings were designed to constantly grow and learn; we sometimes choose to quit learning, hear no further truths; God calls us to continuously grow in faith, to learn how to love better, and to develop in wisdom and in favor with God and other people

Pastoral Prayer

Forgive us, Creator of all, for choosing to close our hearts and minds to the truth you keep revealing to us each new day. Out of fear of challenging a favorite view, we sometimes quit listening and learning; we have even held on to old prejudices in preference to a new revelation you ask us to consider. Like Peter on a balcony, we strive to hang on to old habits that prevent us from hearing a higher truth or a better way. Please teach us how to remain open to your Spirit's constant prodding and pushing us into a deeper faith. Ignite a hunger to grow in grace and understanding each day, and stimulate our imagination to recognize the ever newness of your revelation. Through Christ, your greatest revelation and gift to us, we pray. Amen.

Fifteenth Sunday after Pentecost

Meditation of Preparation

The future often is
In conversation with the past;
Never chained, however, it breathes
Its own crisp air, and moves,
Unfettered, to command its own reward;
We are the children
Of the future, if captured by its vision
And demand—who walk with courage
Into God's unwritten plot!

Call to Leadership and Grace

Leader: God has called us as a people to create a new community.

People: We are a people of heritage and hope, promise and potential, grace and goodness.

Leader: God has chosen us to work in this time and place, for God's kingdom and will to unfold.

People: We have also chosen to embrace this invitation, if we belong to God's family.

Leader: Help us, Lord of the future, to review the past with gratitude and love;

People: Guide us, Good Shepherd, to embrace the future with commitment and purpose,

Leader: That we may do your will as it is in heaven and seek your vision for our lives,

People: That all who see us may see love and grace and peace, as in the face of Christ,

Leader: That we may bear his image, be the presence of a gracious God!

Lead Scripture: Isaiah 43:16-21 and Philippians 3:12-14

Sermon Meditation: "If I Should Die before I Wake"
The God of yesterday also makes things new; we are a people often chained to a "spiritual" past; God invites us into an imaginative spiritual future

Pastoral Prayer

We thank you again for the power of your presence in our spiritual past, Creator God; you made a gracious path for our faith from days gone by to where we stand today; you've placed rich memories of early encounters with you in this community, and in others. Our past is a heritage of treasured experiences that inform our current faith. Assist us now to celebrate our spiritual journey further, to walk with you where you next wish us to develop, and to see the ways we need to add to our community. Guide us to trust you with an unknown tomorrow in which you will stretch and enrich us even more, and call us to embrace the cusp of the next spiritual discovery that will bless and empower us. Through Jesus Christ, our faithful leader, we pray. Amen.

Sixteenth Sunday after Pentecost

Meditation of Preparation

I wear a skeptic's eye
And share the cynic's table;
But don't be quickly fooled—
Beneath the scoffer's voice
Resides a doubting seeker,
Still afraid! Afraid
Of what? Afraid of finding nothing,
And returning, empty handed,
To the stark, unfriendly spaces.

Call to Discovery and Faith

Leader: We have come here to discover, Master of Hope,

People: To discover truths and principles that can shape meaning and hope!

Leader: We have also come to confess: we've lost confidence and focus; belief is distant; faith is far.

People: Help us recall what we are living for, and what is most important;

Leader: Jolt us gently to remember how to find you, and how to be found.

People: Long ago we made promises and made vows that we believed in; help us to believe again!

Leader: We thank you that we need not pretend with you, that we may share what we're not sure of,

People: That you forgive us our frailty, our failures, and our questions.

Leader: Embrace us once again with your unfailing love; strengthen feeble hopes;

People: Renew dreams and purposes, stir new commitments, lead us further into faith and service!

Lead Scripture: Genesis 32:24-29 and John 1:45-51

Sermon Meditation: "Wrestling with God"
The path of faith includes confusion, stress, and disillusionment; it is safe and useful to struggle with our doubts and fears with God; the struggle with our faith and confusion can produce a deeper faith and commitment

Pastoral Prayer

Receive us once again as imperfect and seeking pilgrims on the way, patient God. Our struggles with faith may have more to do with the uncaring and distressing world in which we live than issues with you, we acknowledge. We live with unfairness and injustice at every hand, and peace and trust remain as distant friends. We long for comfort and fulfillment, and too often we struggle with poverty of hope and joy. Teach us, please, how to believe in your care above the carelessness we encounter. Amen.

Seventeenth Sunday after Pentecost

Meditation of Preparation

Benign neglect
Is bound to be
Neither benign nor good!
Distractions that lure me
Away from neighbor, family,
And my better self
Are enemies to my commission;
And will I stand for such neglect?

Call to Awareness and Choice (adapted from 1 John 4:17-21)

Leader: As for us, we know the love God has for us, and we have confidence in it.

People: God is love, and those who continue to love continue in union with God, and God with them.

Leader: Our love will be manifested in all its perfection by our having complete confidence on the day of the judgment;

People: Because just what God is, we also are in the world. Love has in it no element of fear; but perfect love drives away fear,

Leader: Because fear involves pain, and if we give way to pain, there is something imperfect in our love.

People: We love because God first loved us; if we say that we love God, while we hate our neighbor, we are deceivers;

Leader: For if we do not love our neighbor whom we have seen, we cannot love God whom we have not seen.

People: And the command that we have from God is that we who love God must love our fellow human also.

Lead Scripture: Deuteronomy 15:7-11 and Luke 16:19-31

Sermon Meditation: "Overcoming Neglect"
There are many forgotten and neglected children of God in the world; God loves all forgotten and ignored children and wants them cared for and found; as the Body of Christ, we have been commissioned to care for and minister to the forgotten and neglected in our midst

Pastoral Prayer

It's easy to focus entirely on ourselves, God. We worry about our day, and we wonder about our life. We become so consumed with our own needs that we forget about anyone else and their needs. We also compete with others so much that the idea of cooperating to meet someone else's needs is almost counterintuitive. Help us here and now to remember that community is formed in trust and care and that, as followers of Christ, we have a model of service and care for others. Help us tune our hearts and hands to the ministry of seeking out the forgotten and uninvited in our path, that we may offer comfort and compassion to the neglected, and a family of care with whom they can be safe. Forgive us the immaturity that always places ourselves before others, and lead us to understand that we belong to one another, and to you. Teach us to find spiritual maturity, loving God, we pray. Amen.

Eighteenth Sunday after Pentecost

Meditation of Preparation

Someone else is always
Better equipped, or equal
To the challenge; I lag behind,
Off stage, and unimpressed
With my own skills. Does life
Provide the best reward
Only to the gifted—and the dashing?
Or is there satisfaction, even
Recognition—of the average skill?

Call to Worship and Perspective

Leader: We have returned to fill our empty cups with hope, faithful Lord.

People: We've allowed doubt and suspicion to take control of our lives.

Leader: We doubt our skills, question our strengths, fear our visions;

People: We even suspect your intentions, distrust your love, question your methods in a cruel world.

Leader: Restore our faith in ourselves, made in your image, worth being valued!

People: Restore our awareness of your work in us, affirming our importance to you.

Leader: Rekindle our eagerness to learn, to follow, and to believe.

People: Refashion our thoughts to see ourselves, and you, in a new light.

Leader: Enrich our impoverished minds, and clothe our hands with deeds of grace and care,

People: That we may once again reflect the Face of love we know!

Lead Scripture: Judges 6:11-15; Luke 5:4-8; and 1 Corinthians 15:9

Sermon Meditation: "Ordinary People"

The Scriptures affirm God's use of ordinary people in God's mission and work; most of us lead average, ordinary lives and question our worth and value; God reminds us in Jesus Christ that all of us "average" servants are valued, prized, and used by God for good

Pastoral Prayer

We have once again faulted our usefulness and questioned our value in this competitive and isolating world, dear Maker. We struggle to find gifts and skills; we believe others possess far more abilities than we do. We suspect ourselves as unimportant, devalue our contribution to friends, family, and community, and wonder if we make a difference in people's lives. We want to know if you find us useful and valued, good Friend. Since we downplay our skills and talents, we need a strong reminder that we are useful to your purposes and that you have equipped us to be a gift to those we love and to your community of faith. We find it easy to become discouraged, to compare ourselves with others—always with a negative perspective; we screen affirmations and deflect words of encouragement and gratitude. Help us remember that we are made in your image and that our contributions make a difference to you, and to others. In your most holy name we pray. Amen.

Nineteenth Sunday after Pentecost

Meditation of Preparation

Smaller causes
Capture first attention—
Lack imagination; greater purposes
Force evaluation, stir
Concern and passion! How
Are causes chosen? When
Are efforts worthy? When
Is dying for them—valued?
What makes living—better?

Call to Confession and Choice

Leader: Our intentions are pure, but our actions flawed and small, Loving Creator.

People: We promise compassionate deeds and caring words;

Leader: We often deliver vacant words and meager deeds.

People: We pledge ourselves to your purposes and ways,

Leader: But we soon resort to selfish gestures, paltry goals.

People: We thank you again for your presence, which restores our vision;

Leader: For your power, which restores our depleted efforts.

People: We thank you also for the grace of another day, the joy of a deeper purpose,

Leader: The wonder of a generous God!

People: Once again, return into our restless and unimaginative lives, dear Friend!

Lead Scripture: Exodus 3:1-6 and John 3:1-7

Sermon Meditation: "What Will You Give Your Life For?"
There are many causes and missions in which to place our time and energy; some causes and missions are less worthy of our attention;

Christ continually challenges us to choose the same servant causes and mission to which he gave his life

Pastoral Prayer

We find so many ways to spend our time, dear One, and often are distracted by self-serving and secondary enterprises. Help us to hear your beckoning voice above the noise of lesser invitations. Teach us to discern missions and causes that you embrace, and to give ourselves unstintingly to issues and concerns you believe in, that we may be about your business here on earth. Forgive us also for the preoccupations that sometimes derail the useful investment of our time in your worthy work of healing and guiding. Reset our minds to higher tasks that reflect your love for each of us, and ignite a spirit of compassion and attention to what you deem important and best. Through Jesus Christ, our Savior and guide, we pray. Amen.

Twentieth Sunday after Pentecost (Reformation Sunday)

Meditation of Preparation

How am I judged?
What is the measure
By which I'm evaluated? How
Does the Keeper of the tally—
Keep the tally?
Is it a matter of behavior—
Or a matter of the heart?

Call to Faith and Responsibility

Leader: Re-form our lives, Lord of Creation and Judgment:

People: Re-form our hopes, worn and damaged in the stress of life;

Leader: Re-form our vision, blurred and blunted by exposure to compromise;

People: Re-form our focus, bruised and battered by conflicting values.

Leader: Renew us, God of new beginnings:

People: Restore purpose and perspective, teaching us to love in us what Christ loves;

Leader: Renew the peace that lifts our hearts and minds to see your way and will;

People: Renew the joy that overcomes our burdens, the love that overrides each sorrow,

Leader: That we may become reformers who refurbish your will on earth each day

People: And work your changeless love and grace into this changing world!

Lead Scripture: 1 Kings 8:15-19 and Romans 2:26-29

Sermon Meditation: "A Matter of the Heart?"
Our lives are evaluated daily as to purpose and effect; we are in need of grace for actions and thoughts that fall short of God's design; God frees us in forgiveness to rise up and follow Christ's heart, standards, and actions

Pastoral Prayer

Sometimes we are unaware of having failed or sinned, merciful Savior. Sometimes we are fully aware that we have chosen poorly, selfishly, thoughtlessly. Forgive us for the irresponsible discipleship we model, re-clothe us in your purposes and actions, and stretch our capacity to do justice and mercy and kindness. Reduce the anxieties and preoccupations that prevent our understanding of your guidance in our daily labor. Bring clarity to our confusion, compassion to our detachment, care to our carelessness. Light a flame within us that makes us attractive to your cause and leads us to places and people where we may carry your good news. With trust in your most holy and superior ways, we pray. Amen.

Twenty-first Sunday after Pentecost

Meditation of Preparation

People and places
Hold their secrets,
Waiting for the moment
To reveal their wares;
Travelers on the journey
Either pay attention,
Or forfeit the disclosure
Of a lifetime!
Will I seize the day
Or miss the revelation?

Call to Awareness and Grace

Leader: We have returned as eager pilgrims on a journey with you, Revealing God.

People: We are seekers often unaware of seeking because we are incomplete and fallible.

Leader: On our own we stray, stumble, struggle in your care.

People: We learn, remember, heal, and follow.

Leader: Teach us to learn from children and adults, believers and seekers,

People: Poor and rich, humble and proud, friend and stranger.

Leader: Help us in worship to remember your love for us in difficult places,

People: Your presence in joyful times, your care at every intersection!

Leader: Forgive us the temptation to retain our wounds, resist your healing power.

People: Help us watch for new revelations; nurture and feed us, still surprise and heal us.

Leader: Embrace and renew us, that we may with confidence enjoy the present moment,

All: Let go of the past, embrace the future, and listen for your voice at every turn!

Lead Scripture: Genesis 18:1-5 and Hebrews 13:1-2

Sermon Meditation: "Strangers as Angels"

God starts conversations with us at unexpected moments in unpredictable relationships; God's invitation is to a spiritual adventure and a deeper faith; when we pay attention to everyday encounters, we can discover the presence and call of God in our lives

Pastoral Prayer

Dear God of the desert and the mountaintop, we give you thanks for holy moments when we suddenly discover your presence and movement in our lives. Stir our imagination and capacity to listen and recognize your call and companionship throughout our daily walk. Help us learn at crucial intersections on the road, and gain your guidance and revelation in the silence. Forgive us for presupposing that we're not useful to your mission. Transform our plans to meet your will. Awaken dormant skills and dreams that need reviving within us, and offer focus and courage in the broken places. You have sought us before; seek us again, for we have sometimes wandered far away—and cannot find a way back. Thank you for choosing us, gracious God; reassure us that we are valued in spite of our imperfections. In the name of the One who can redeem us and bless us and who seeks us out, we pray. Amen.

Twenty-second Sunday after Pentecost

Meditation of Preparation

How is a dream advanced?
How is a goal achieved?
How is a purpose tamed and clothed
And made to live a truth?

Our dreams are born, and live
By our determination
And commitment to a cause!
To what endeavors
Will I choose to give myself?

Call to Gratitude and Commitment (for a Stewardship Sunday)

Leader: We have been given much, Generous God.

People: We have often wasted and misused what you've given us to use.

Leader: We confess that we stress about our own welfare and are distracted by our own needs.

People: We've come to ask for a vision that seeks beyond self-satisfaction.

Leader: We ask for the courage and satisfaction that comes even to the place of sacrifice.

People: We ask for wisdom to be responsible with the immense resources you have shared with us.

Leader: Renew our sight to see the world through your eyes;

People: Reset our hearts to feel the joy and passion of your giving ways;

All: Retool our choices to join the richness of your plans on earth!

Lead Scripture: Exodus 36:2-7 and 1 Peter 4:10-11

Sermon Meditation: "The Secret of Generosity"

God's example is our model for giving generously and sharing from an overflow of gifts; fear of want and anxiety about our own needs interfere with our willingness to give; one of the greatest secrets of personal fulfillment and joy comes in our sharing generously from our provision

Pastoral Prayer

You have empowered us and trusted us with much in your earthly garden, dear Master Gardener. You invited us in, first, to partake of and enjoy the bounty of your love as a diversity of fruit and fauna. When we failed you, you returned and helped us start over, providing food and shelter in the home you gave us on this planet; then you asked us to share from the overflow of our plenty for the care and sustenance of others, and we have often been so consumed by our fears of not having enough that we have hoarded more than we have need for, rather than sharing it. Teach us again the value of offering from our overflow—and your generosity—so that we also may be blessed by the gentle fulfillment of witnessing that others have enough! Remind us that, made in your image, we are most at peace and in greatest joy when we share with one another and with you. Heal our anxieties, we pray; transform our self-focused lives into tender instruments of your grace and compassion, that we may encourage and embrace others, as you have encouraged us and called us into the beauty of your way of life! Through Christ, we pray. Amen.

The Twenty-third Sunday after Pentecost (Christ the King Sunday, Thanksgiving Week)

Meditation of Preparation

The truth at first
Is judgment to our ears;
But truth is also
The bearer of good news:
If we turn and abide
Within the truth,
Then listen, and follow,
The truth will set us free!

Responsive Call to Gratitude and Grace (Congregation and Choir)

Leader: We've come to give you thanks for finding us when we have strayed, dear God.

Choir: We thank you, Lord; Lord, we thank you.

People: You walked into our loneliness and struggle, Lord;

Choir: We thank you, Lord; Lord, we thank you.

People: You have rescued from stingy thoughts, unworthy goals, misguided priorities;

Choir: We thank you, Lord; Lord, we thank you.

People: You have given us a world of choices, a multitude of joys, a lavish set of dreams!

Choir: Lord, we thank you; we thank you, Lord.

People: You've provided us a garden to live in, friends and family to live with and love, purposes to live by;

Choir: We thank you, Lord; Lord, we thank you.

People: With deep-felt gratitude, we stand amazed at your creation and at the extravagance of your love in Jesus Christ!

Choir: We thank, Lord; Lord, we thank, you. Amen.

Lead Scripture: Daniel 7:13-14 and John 18:36-37

Sermon Meditation: "Listening to the Truth: Judgment and Hope"
God has designed a high standard for discipleship; God's truth as standards for believers finds us always wanting; the God of mercy evokes profound gratitude, because in Jesus Christ we are declared both forgiven and loved by God

Pastoral Prayer

We've once again become aware of our shortcomings and our sin, Maker of High Standards! Your ways are not our ways, and we shudder at the possibility that your judgment might pronounce us unfit for service—and for discipleship. Yet you have again reassured us in Jesus Christ that your aim and purpose is *not* to condemn but to save us—and to challenge us to live the abundant life you envisioned for us. Our hearts rejoice with your grace; gratitude is a small fraction of our response to your forgiveness and care. We are today reminded again that you created all that we have for our joy, and that you created us to multiply your love, and that you constantly redeem and salvage what we destroy in our failure to do your will! Accept, then, again, our heartfelt thanksgiving for your generosity and mercy toward us—now, and always. In the name of your Son Jesus Christ, our Redeemer and Savior, we pray. Amen.

www.ingramcontent.com/pod-product-compliance
Lightning Source LLC
Chambersburg PA
CBHW060519090426
42735CB00011B/2299